THE NERD & THE QUARTERBACK

A JACKSON HIGH NOVEL

M.L. COLLINS

YOU'VE GOT THIS, ALI FROST

Ali

2ND QUARTER BEGINS, OCT 7, 7:35 A.M.

Please excuse Ali's absence due to a surprise alien abduction.

Probably not a good excuse.

Holding my hand out over the vent, I let the cool air flow against my palm and between my fingers while possible excuses for skipping school ran through my head. I picked up my lucky Black Widow ball—the one my Nana left me in her will—moved onto the approach, and took my stance.

Ali was absent from school because her emotional support goldfish died.

Eh...maybe my lame excuses were a sign I shouldn't skip. Although, it wasn't like anyone would miss me.

"This tune goes out to Ali Frost." The announcement echoed over the PA system just before "I Will Survive" pumped throughout Bowl-O-Rama along with a "Go, Ali!" and a "Hooah!" from the Flying Aces down on lane seven.

"Thanks, Mr. Jones!" I called out, keeping my attention

focused on the ball in my hand and the lane stretched out in front of me.

Ali missed school due to car trouble which sparked a migraine which caused the need for a mental health day. Oh, and cramps.

Overkill? Yeah. Okay, if I get a strike I'll skip. Straight wrist, eyes on target, steps, swing, slide-step, throw, release, follow-through, aaand… Nope. Too much spin. My ball shot down the oiled lane toward my target veering millimeters off course. I didn't need to watch the pins fly from the crash of my ball to know it wasn't a strike. 7-10 split. *Bed Posts.*

Dang it. What about…

Ali didn't make it to school because even four hundred eighty-five revolutions of the sun after her personal ground zero she is still gutted, empty, angry, bereft, pathetic, and prefers Bowl-O-Rama to her new high school.

Maybe not that one either. I doubted Principal Barstow would go for it even though it was the truth.

I'd much rather hang out here all day. Bowl-O-Rama had become my safe space and escape hatch. I didn't used to come to the alley in the morning. Insomnia changed that. There were only two places to go at five a.m. in our small town: Waffle House or Bowl-O-Rama. Bowl-O-Rama was practically my second home.

"Ali," Mr. Jones called over the PA again. "Your dad called. Said to tell you to get your ass to school."

I flipped around, arching an eyebrow at Mr. Jones standing behind the shoe rental counter. My dad would not have said "ass." A year ago, sure, but not now. Not since he quit his job last year to be Mr. Mom.

"So, I put it into my own words." He shrugged and gave me a wink. "Same gist. Skedaddle, girl. Get outta here. It's your senior year. Shouldn't you be more excited?"

"This is my excited face." I grabbed my ball off the return rack and gave it a quick wipe with my towel before sliding it

2

into the bag. After changing my shoes, I swung my backpack over one shoulder, grabbed my bowling ball bag, and headed out. "I'll see you tomorrow morning, you know."

"Don't think I won't tell your father if you skip school." He pointed at me. "I will be extremely disappointed if I see your face before three o'clock when school lets out."

"Sorry, not sorry, Mr. J. I've got bowling class first period this quarter. You're stuck with me."

He shook his head. "You need to get out more. Hang out with your friends."

"You guys *are* my friends."

"That's sad. I mean, we like you, but you need to hang out with people who aren't drawing social security or buying adult diapers, you know?" Mr. J's bushy gray eyebrows lowered over his piercing blue eyes. "You need to get a life."

No kidding. For the past year, I'd fantasized about future-me living a kick-ass life some place where high school football wasn't a thing and Sour Patch Kids grew on trees. But the sad truth was present-me was stuck right here in Devil's Lap, Texas. So, not future-me yet but—silver linings!—not past-me either.

I would get a life, just as soon as I could kick the small town dirt from my Chuck Taylor's. I hated the thought of leaving my dad alone, but it had been over a year since our lives imploded and he needed to get a life too.

I pushed through the front doors and out into the bright morning sunlight. Since skipping wasn't an option, it was off to school for me. All I had to do was make it through the rest of my senior year of high school.

Ten minutes later, I pulled Milo, my fifteen-year-old Volvo with sun-faded teal paint, into my assigned space with time to spare before the first bell rang. I shut off Milo's engine and closed my eyes and counted. *One. Two.* On cue Milo's horn—a mooing cow—sounded. The cow horn was on account of my nana's quirky personality. The fact that it mooed every time I

3

shut off the engine was on account of Bubba. That being Bubba of Bubba's Horns and Hooters.

It was a well-known fact that Bubba was like a T.V. with only one channel and even that channel had bad reception. But Nana and Bubba's grandma had been good friends and she'd insisted Bubba was her horn guy. Did I cringe every time I turned off my car? Yes. But I also sent up a little prayer of thanks that Bubba wasn't a brain surgeon.

I chewed on my bottom lip as I sat watching the parking lot fill up. I wasn't new here. I'd spent almost half of last year at Jackson. But a new quarter meant new classes and new classes meant new kids to deal with. Have you ever walked across a lawn in Texas? Where fire ant mounds sit like hidden landmines in the tall grass? You had to be on guard with every anxiety-building step. Cue the Jaws music. That was me entering a new classroom.

I pulled out my phone, held it in front of me, and hit the video record.

"This is it. One semester down; three to go. Anxiety level: about a four. Today's objective: make it through the day. I'm so close to closing the book on this ugly chapter of my life. Stay focused. Ignore everything else. Positive affirmation: I rely on myself. I do not need other people for happiness.

"It doesn't matter what other kids think. I like myself and that's enough." I pointed at my image on the phone. "You've got this, Ali Frost."

Clicking to stop the recording, I uploaded it to my video diary. Yeah, I'd rolled my eyes when the therapist had recommended keeping a diary. Writing wasn't my thing, plus it was weird. Why would I want to keep a daily chronicle of the worst year of my life? I'd promised my dad I'd go along with the therapy sessions, so I compromised and started a vlog. And maybe the therapist knew a thing or two because it was helping.

It didn't feel as awkward as talking to myself in my bathroom mirror.

The muted warning bell sounded from inside the concrete jungle. Time to stop stalling. I made my way inside the way I always did which was part SWAT team and part hiding in plain sight: hug the edges, focus on what's in front of me, and avoid eye contact. In one sense, it was easy to disappear. Kids were happy to let you. They'd look right through you, walk around you, sit in class with you for months and never notice you. Being invisible was my safe harbor until I could sail toward a new horizon.

Going ghost wasn't my natural tendency. I wasn't an introvert. In fact, for most of my life I'd been a happy, outgoing, confident girl. Crazy how fast things can change. Which reminded me, I needed to stop by the counseling office during lunch today.

I tossed my lunch into my locker and grabbed out a spiral, leafing through it to see if it had enough empty pages to reuse for the new quarter, but no. Too many pages filled with angsty doodles, so I slid it back in and grabbed another. This one was practically new.

"Whoa, get a load of Clark today," some guy said, his voice booming loudly from the lockers behind me.

I flinched knowing what was coming. Like a pack of lions, they'd singled out the weakest in a herd and had begun the attack. My hypothalamus went into overdrive, shooting adrenaline through my veins. My heart rate spiked, my lungs sucked in oxygen, and my muscles tensed. All systems go; ready for fight or flight. Except, not really. Maybe my ancient ancestors were kick-ass ninja Neanderthals who'd chosen to fight, but not me. Not after the last year. My instinct was to flee. To escape, scamper, skedaddle, rabbit, bolt.

The problem was Clark was Rowena Clark, one of the girls

on my bowling team. A nice girl who'd never hurt anyone. We may not be friends, but I couldn't desert her.

"Clark, dress like a nerd day was yesterday. Although I guess every day is dress like a nerd day for you."

Jerk. Just because it was a lame insult didn't mean it hurt any less. Not when kids shot insults like arrows at you all day long. I had to do something. But what?

If I confronted the dude, I'd be in his sights. Thank you, but no. Although...maybe I didn't need to confront him. I just needed him to leave. *Right.* I tore a page from my spiral, slid a pen from my backpack, and jotted out a short note.

The jerk's jerky sidekick thought his friend was hilarious and barked out a laugh.

"Clark the aardvark. I didn't think it was possible but your nose grew even more overnight."

Just like a bully: find a kid's Achilles' heel and poke at it with glee.

I folded the note in half and turned toward the conversation. Rowena stood at her locker, her shoulders hunched forward protectively and her hand shaking as she dialed in her combination.

"Hey." Avoiding eye contact, I shoved the note at the guy who'd started it. "Some cheerleader told me to give this to you."

"Who?" he asked as he unfolded the paper and read.

"I don't know. Pretty. Long, dark brown hair..."

"Was it Tiffany Peters?" The dude asked, still looking at the note only now with a huge I'm-hotter-than-Chris Hemsworth smirk. Ha!

"Um, big blue eyes?" I took a wild guess.

"No. Brown," he said.

"Oh, yes! Exactly. Big brown eyes—"

"Big rack? Nice badonkadonk?"

Literally had to bite my tongue. Guess "Big brain? Nice personality?" was a bridge too far for this gronk-nugget.

"Dude," his friend punched him in the shoulder. "I bet it's Jodi Ball."

"Yaaassss. I knew she was checking me out at soccer practice." His smirk got smirkier. "Jodi Ball wants me bad."

I deserved a medal for holding back an eye roll.

"You should go," I prodded, sending up a silent apology to Jody Ball. "Now. Before she gets bored waiting for you. There's a wide selection at the Jocks-R-Us store."

"Yeah. Oh, yeah." He turned and ran down the hall, his friend trailing after him.

Rowena released a loud breath. "Thanks, Ali."

"Hey, no one messes with a bowling teammate and gets away with it." I closed my locker, giving the lock a random spin.

"Actually, it h-happens all the time." Rowena pushed her glasses up with the touch of her finger at the bridge. "I get too nervous to d-defend myself let alone anyone else, so I really appreciate it."

"Anytime." Either way—whether you attempted to ignore the bullies or confronted them—it took nerves of steel. Ask me how I know?

2

NOBODY PUTS BABY IN THE CORNER BOOTH

Ali

COUNSELING OFFICE, "A" LUNCH, 11:34 A.M.

I was in the middle of taking advice from a pair of imaginary rabbits when a deep voice interrupted.

"Hey."

I turned my attention from the "Hop into the Future with the Jackson Jackalopes" poster in the counseling office over to the open door where high school royalty, our star quarterback, stood. Dax DeLeon couldn't be talking to me.

"How's it going?" he said with a nod.

"You can see me?" Oh heck, I'd said that out loud. In this case, my surprise was understandable since usually no one in the "it" crowd noticed me. Which was exactly how I liked it.

"Do you think you're invisible?" His eyebrows rose into the sun-streaked shaggy brown hair falling across his forehead. "Is that why you're here for counseling?"

I narrowed my eyes at him and he shrugged and leaned against the wall. I was busy deciding if I wanted to bother responding to him when P3 stuck her head into the office.

"Who are you talking to?" Perfect Popular Paige asked Dax. No question Paige was the most popular girl in school. She was pretty. She was a cheerleader. Duh. The fact that her father was the baseball coach gave her some extra clout. Like she needed it.

He slid his glance from Paige over to me. So of course, Paige's attention whipped my way.

Gee thanks, quarterback dude. I didn't want to be on anyone's radar. Especially not hers. I'd arrived at Jackson in the middle of junior year last year and done my best to keep to my own little orbit. Not that many kids were eager to open their cliques to let the new awkward girl in.

Okay, that wasn't fair. The girls on the bowling team had tried to be friends, but having been stabbed in the back by friends I thought I could count on… No. Call me crazy, but I'd have to be a masochist to volunteer for that again.

"Come on, Dax." Paige tossed her long blond hair. "We're all going to Randy's for lunch."

He held up a yellow appointment slip for her to see. "Can't. My schedule's messed up."

"Oh! I'll wait with you so you're not bored sitting here alone," she said.

Dax's eyes flicked over to me.

I arched an eyebrow at him.

He frowned and his gaze took me in in all my quirky glory. From my two braids—the best way to control my wild curls—down to my baggy jeans and my aqua Chuck Taylor high tops.

"I'm not alone," he said, waving his hand in my direction. "I'm with…with…"

Uh huh. I crossed my arms over my chest and waited because he'd proven my point. Invisible.

"Frosty? You're telling me you're turning me down for her?"

"Frosty?" he asked me.

I stared at him without replying. First, because I hated the nickname I'd been assigned. It was low-hanging fruit as my last name was Frost. It hadn't taken many brain cells for some kid to come up with that one. Second, Dax DeLeon was easy to stare at and probably used to it. The guy was gorgeous. If a girl liked bad-boy jocks too hot for mere mortal girls like me.

He was hot...from his sneakers with some famous athlete's name on them to his long muscular legs encased in perfectly-faded blue jeans...okay, I got hung up on his thighs, but, trust me, the rest was good too. Just go look up "hot jock" in the dictionary; it's sure to have his picture.

"But, baby..."

Dax shook his head, his eyes still holding mine.

Something about his cockiness ruffled my feathers.

"Baby?" I asked, tilting my head, giving it right back to him. There was an awkward silence with Paige waiting for Dax to look at her but Dax's gaze was fixed on me. What was his problem?

I met him stare for stare, hoping he'd get bored and I could go back to blending into the background but nope, still he stood with all his attention focused on me like I was Tom Brady scoring a Hail Mary touchdown with three seconds to go in the game. Was he trying to make Paige jealous? The two of them were an item last year. Were they in some fight? Ha! Like I wanted to be dragged into their drama. No thanks. I frowned at him and his lips tilted up into a crooked grin.

"Baby, we always go to Randy's. Pizza in our corner booth. Everyone will be there."

"Not me. I've got to get Boyd to fix my schedule." He settled into the chair next to me, looking like he wasn't going anywhere.

"Nobody puts Baby in the corner booth," I said and got two pairs of clueless eyes on me. Only Mrs. G, the secretary, snickered from behind her desk. "Thank you, Mrs. G. My generation has no respect for the classics."

Paige gave me her "please go catch some Pokémon in traffic" look. Only the look didn't come close to saying "please."

Whatever. I focused on the printed schedule in my hands, smoothing the corner that had crinkled from being crammed into my backpack. I did *not* have to make a schedule change. No, I had to have my quarterly "make sure Ali is fine" talk with Dr. Boyd. Which I hated, but it gave my dad some peace of mind so I put up with it.

"Dax—"

"Just go to lunch. I'll catch everyone later," he said, his deep voice firm.

"Sure, okay. I'll see you later." I wasn't looking at Paige, but her voice came out tentative and soft, like if a kitten with big, blinking eyes could talk it would sound just like her.

The small reception area went quiet except for Mrs. G's nails clicking away on her computer keyboard. Figuring the coast was clear, I lifted my head only to find Dax leaning casually into my space, his gaze moving over my schedule. Ha! Bet he was trying to find out my name.

I jerked my schedule from his line of sight, slipping it inside my backpack on the floor before sitting back, keeping my gaze far away from Dax and firmly on Mrs. G's fast-moving hands. She had her nails professionally manicured every week with fun colors and themes throughout the school year. Looked like she'd gone with the school colors this week: blue and silver.

"Nice school spirit, Mrs. G."

"Thank you, Ali." She paused her typing, stretching a hand out and wiggling her fingers for me to see. "I even got rabbit decals."

"You really ramped it up a notch." Rabbit. Mythical Jackalope. Close enough, especially because our school mascots, Mr. and Ms. Jackalope, were long-eared rabbits. What were the odds Mrs. G was a former cheerleader?

"So…" Dax's voice interrupted my ignoring him. I kept my gaze on Mrs. G's hands. "Your name's Ali."

I gave him the side-eye. Why was he still talking to me now that Paige was gone?

"Why does everyone call you Frosty?" He leaned forward, invading my space and shoving himself into my line of sight, making it impossible to pretend he wasn't sitting next to me talking.

"Newsflash: everyone doesn't." Like Paige and her crowd was everyone. And her crowd was his crowd. I guess to him he meant everyone who mattered. I honestly didn't know Dax DeLeon at all, but he was sounding like a douche canoe. Which would make it a lot easier to resist his beautiful dark brown eyes and hot smile. In theory anyway. "Just the ones who feel the need to belittle others to make themselves feel better."

Mrs. G coughed but kept on typing and I kept on ignoring Dax while he kept on looking at me. (Just a guess since I refused to look at him, but that would explain why the left side of my face felt like I'd sunbathed in Del Rio in August. At noon. Without sunscreen.) Thankfully, Dr. Boyd's door finally opened.

"Dottie, would you adjust the numbers on the hall bulletin board of available electives? We're down to three open spots in bowling and two in life skills. Auto and wood working slots are the same."

"Absolutely."

"Come on in, Ms. Frost." Dr. Boyd lowered his wire-frame glasses down his nose to look at Dax. "Mr. DeLeon, why are you here?"

"Just need a quick schedule change, if you have the time now." Dax stood up, sliding in front of me. "Is that okay, Ali? Unless you needed to talk about that invisible thing with him. You should definitely go first if that's the case."

"Darn, you can still see me." I didn't want the attention of Dax and his crowd. I could handle being laughed at by the popular kids, but that didn't mean I wanted to. It would be an annoying distraction. To be honest, with the way the last year had gone, there were days when I felt like someone had opened the top of my head, filled it with diet soda, dropped in a handful of Mentos, and slammed it closed. If I had to deal with kids like Dax and Paige, you might as well shake me up and get the explosion over with.

"Ali?" Dr. Boyd asked. "His schedule change will only take a minute."

"Sure. Whatever." It wasn't like I needed to hurry to an off-campus lunch at Randy's with the cool kids. No, I'd sit out on one of the benches under the live oaks eating my bag lunch near the other happily weird loners in school. But it still annoyed me that Dax assumed his need was more important than mine. Maybe it was, but Dax DeLeon didn't know that.

I stifled a sigh and slumped back into my chair as Dax enjoyed the red-carpet treatment from Dr. Boyd. I guess when you're the star quarterback and the hottest guy on campus, you get used to the world revolving around you. Man, I couldn't wait to get out of this place and into a world where my destiny wasn't decided by some anointed clique of kids with the most "likes."

"Chin up, Ali. Life after high school is very different." Mrs. G gave me a soft smile and went back to her keyboard.

"That's what I'm clinging to, Mrs. G." Like a raft in the middle of a stormy sea. I was counting down the days. Literally.

My gaze drifted back to the poster. Mr. and Ms. Jackalope were giving bad advice. Hopping into the future was too painfully slow. I wanted to sprint into the future at full speed to get out of here faster.

Dr. Boyd's inner-office door opened and Dax came strolling out.

"See you around," he said, throwing me a wink on his way past.

"Doubt it." I'd managed to avoid that whole clique of kids so far and planned on keeping it that way. #HeadDown #WorkHard #GoalOriented #HappyLoner

"Hey, Ali..." Dax paused before leaving the office, his hand on the outer office door handle and his dark eyes freezing me in my tracks halfway toward Dr. Boyd's office.

"What, DeLeon?" I was going for impatient, but, sadly, I sounded a bit breathless and curious even to my own ears. Because the sad reality was I wasn't immune to bad-boy jocks too hot for a nerd like me.

"Newsflash: you're not invisible anymore." He winked at me. "I see you."

3

IMPROVISE ON THE FLY

Dax

I left the counseling office grinning, feeling like when I ran a successful scramble play for the go-ahead touchdown in a game.

Life was a lot like football. As a quarterback, I practiced and prepared to run all the planned plays to win the game. But because life—like football—never goes according to plan, sometimes a guy had to improvise on the fly. A new opportunity opened up—and in a split second you had to decide to take it or let it go.

That was what I'd just done. To what purpose? Honestly, no idea, but I saw the opportunity and something in my gut said to grab it with both hands. At the very least, it would make this semester more interesting.

Not to be cocky or anything, but most girls giggled and fluttered their eyelashes when I met them. None of them gave me a quirked eyebrow and sarcasm. *Baby?* I was intrigued. Not that I was looking to start something. I wasn't. Being with Paige last year had sucked up too much of my attention. There was too much drama in a relationship. It had been a big distraction—a distraction I couldn't afford.

My teammates counted on me and I'd let them down last season. I'd earned the starting quarterback role after a stellar sophomore year. Last year, my play was pretty solid, up until post-season. Which was why this year I needed—and planned—to be at the top of my game. For my teammates and for the college scouts.

So, no relationships for me this football season. But that didn't mean I couldn't have fun, even if was just to get a rise out of Ali Frost once a day.

"Dax! Hold up!"

I turned at my friend TJ's voice. TJ Devlin and I had given each other busted lips in some playground fight in third grade and been best friends ever since.

"You heading to Randy's?" He slammed his locker closed and swung his backpack over one shoulder before joining me.

"Not feeling Randy's today, you know?" He knew. He knew I'd ended things with Paige at the beginning of summer. He also knew Paige had convinced herself we were just "on a break" and had been trying to get back together ever since.

"I hear you. Come on. Let's hit up the cafeteria."

"On second thought…" I paused, weighing which would be worse: crappy cafeteria food or having Paige hanging on me and acting like we were still together. "We could sneak into the teacher's lounge and grab something from their fridge."

"And risk detention?" TJ gave my shoulder a push down the hall. "At least if we get sick, we'll be sick together."

"Quit pushing me, Devlin, or I'm going to tell coach I'm too hurt to practice. Then you'll be in big trouble."

"Oooh, I'm scared." He wasn't. Mostly because he knew I was BSing. It would have to be a huge deal to rat on a friend. But also, because Coach was TJ's uncle. Coach Devlin had been a star quarterback for the Cowboys. In college he missed the

Heisman by a few votes but I was fairly certain the huge, shiny Super Bowl ring he wore took the sting out of that.

Folks around town said Coach Devlin would have been a Hall of Fame player, if that one tackle hadn't blown his knee and ended his career a decade too early. I'd watched all the films from his college and professional games and I had to agree. Jackson High School was darn lucky he decided to come back home and coach.

Heck, I was darn lucky he did and I had TJ to thank for that. Why else would some famous jock who dated models and Hollywood starlets turn down a broadcasting job rumored to have paid more than his QB salary for small town Texas? I figured to coach TJ.

"Whoa, what is that glorious smell?" TJ asked, twisting his head around toward the cafeteria with its sea of white tables and high school kids hungry enough to eat the close imitation they passed off as actual food. "Is it just me, or do you smell—?"

"Tamales." My mouth watered just thinking about scarfing down four of them. I sniffed the air again. "Really good tamales. I swear those smell like my abuelita's."

"Dax! Dax! I did it! Come see!"

I recognized Kev's voice right away. I zipped my gaze around until I spotted him. He stood—more like hopped from foot to foot—with a mega-watt smile on his face, waving his hand frantically in the air while the lunch ladies beamed at him from behind the stainless-steel counter.

Now, the fact that Kev was smiling and excited was nothing new. Kev was the student manager for the football and lacrosse teams and just about the most school-spirited student in school. Well, maybe it was a tie between him and Lacey Trueheart, president of the pep club, but I was pretty sure he even had Lacey beat.

TJ and I walked over to the food line, the spicy aroma getting stronger and more mouthwatering with each step.

"Look, Dax! Look what Kev did." Kev stepped to the side, revealing a sweet looking lunch buffet. Tamales, rice, corn and black beans salad, chips, and all the fixings. "Your grandma's tamales."

I pulled my gaze from the tray of corn husk wrapped tamales and the smiling lunch ladies lined up ready to serve and over to Kev. "Your senior project? You finished it already?"

"Almost. Twenty-four recipes from students approved by Mrs. Avila. Principal Barstow said the cafeteria will use one every Wednesday. Three to go." Kev frowned over the missing three. "There are twenty-seven Wednesdays left this year. Twenty-seven minus twenty-four equals three. Kev needs three more recipes. Three more. Three more to finish."

"You'll get them. Probably today once kids try the tamales and see how cool this is," I said. "Kev, this is fantastic."

"High five fantastic?" he asked, his eyes going even bigger as he held his palm up for me.

"Heck yes," I said, and we high fived then did a fist bump for good measure.

"This is awesome, Kev." TJ and Kev did the same high five, fist bump routine much to Kev's excitement. "No one will want to go off campus for lunch on Wednesdays, that's for sure."

"Yay me!" Kev pumped both fists in the air over his head before turning to the buffet. "Let's eat, guys."

"You first, Kev." I handed him a plastic tray from the stack next to the long stainless-steel counter before grabbing one for myself. Together we slid our divided trays down the line, watching with greedy eyes as the lunch ladies scooped food onto them.

I sat at the nearest available table, totally messing up the normal hierarchy of who sits where, because I didn't want to walk another foot before getting the tamales into my stomach. TJ and Kev sat and the table quickly filled up with kids, mostly from the team, attacking the food like bears on a picnic basket. My abuelita's tamales were the best.

"Mmmm," TJ said before shoving his face back into his plate of food. "Mmhm hmmm mmmm."

"Right? Kev, I vote you get an A+ for your project. It was genius." I grabbed my milk, pulled the spout open, and drank it down. "What's on the menu next week?"

"Lacey Trueheart's dad's veggie tofu stir fry."

"Oh." My excitement level for Kev's Wednesday menu plummeted over a cliff. I'd eaten tofu once when my mom had tried to sneak it into a recipe. I grimaced at the memory.

"No, Dax. It's good. I swear on the Jackson Jackalope playbook." Kev held his palm up next to his head. "I taste-tested every recipe."

"Then I'm looking forward to it," I said, but my attention snagged on a girl walking by. Ali Frost walked behind Kev, dropped a Twinkie next to his tray, high fived the hand Kev lifted over his head without a pause, like relay runners passing a baton, and she kept right on walking—not sparing me or any of the other guys a glance. Huh.

I watched her walk away, her copper-colored hair hung in two long braids. Not a style many girls wore around school. Then again neither were her clothes, but that only made her stand out more. Funny that I hadn't been aware of Ali Frost before but now that I'd seen her, I couldn't help noticing her. Especially when she looked at me in Boyd's office, hitting me with a pair of the lightest green eyes I'd ever seen.

"You'll like it," Kev said, tearing open the Twinkie and taking a big bite. "You too, TJ."

"Kev, you know Ali?" I asked, causing TJ's head to swivel sharply around to me. Just because I'd sworn all summer long that my plan was to stay single and make football my singular focus, didn't mean I couldn't get a little more information. It wasn't very often that a girl could care less when I talked to her, and I was curious.

"Sure. Ali gives Kev Twinkies," Kev said.

"Why does she give you Twinkies?"

"Because she likes the Kev. And Kev likes Twinkies." He was happily licking the last of the cream filling off his fingers.

"Why are you asking about Frosty?" TJ asked.

"Her name's Ali. She doesn't like being called Frosty."

TJ cocked an eyebrow.

"It's no big deal. I've never seen her before today and she's...different."

"Different how? I mean, she's way different from Paige if that's what you're getting at."

"I don't know. Just different." Night and day from Paige and the other girls in our circle of friends. Most of my close friends were teammates since we spent hours and hours on the field together. Football players and cheerleaders always went together like Texas and cowboy boots. But something about Ali and her couldn't-care-less attitude grabbed my attention and wouldn't let go.

"Dude, no girls, all game." TJ frowned and shook his head. "Does that ring a bell? We made a pact. You've got scouts to razzle-dazzle. Not to mention the rest of us are kind of counting on you to carry us to the state championship."

"I know. That's still the plan." College scouts and the state championship. Right. I was throwing everything I had into football this season.

Ali Frost was simply a puzzle that needed solving. That was all.

4

PREDATORS, SCAVENGERS & HERBIVORES. OH MY.

Ali

Student Parking Lot, Oct 8, 7:47 a.m.

"Forty-seven days down. One hundred thirty-nine to go." I sat in my car talking into the video of my phone for my diary. "Anxiety level: two. Today's goal: Avoid DeLeon and his crowd. Also, I've got to do something about Dad. There's no way I can go away to college and leave him alone the way he is now. I'll have to figure something out. Positive affirmation: This day will bring me nothing but joy."

Maybe joy was pushing it a little but whatever. I did like that I had bowling class first period. It meant I could park Milo, sit listening to music until the first period bell rang, and head right to the activity bus. It let me put off dealing with the gauntlet of judgy upper-tier kids in the social hierarchy. Aka the hallways.

In case you never went to public high school (you lucky thing you), here are the tiers:

First Tier: Predators. At the top of the high school food chain are the carnivores. The lions, grizzlies, and sharks. Beautiful but sometimes deadly.

Second Tier: Scavengers. They lie immediately below the predators. These are the kids who hang out on the outskirts of the popular crowd trying to get in. Like vultures, they live off the meager scraps the popular kids leave behind or on a lucky day toss their way. A few dung beetles in here too.

Third Tier: Secondary Consumers. Snakes. Snakes are rare. See * below.

Fourth Tier: Herbivores: Nerds and bowlers (but I repeat myself) are one level above algae. This is the peaceful, minding-our-own-business and just-trying to-survive layer. Think deer, mice, bunnies, and even elephants. Our goal is to survive high school. We stay alert, trying to dodge the carnivores and snakes. Survival tactics include blending into the background, hiding or burrowing. The foremost goal for my social tier is to avoid being the chum in a feeding frenzy. Trust me when I say you do not want to be chum. It's vicious and painful.

Bottom Tier: Grass, algae and bacteria. These are the stoners. They sort of exist seemingly doing nothing. They don't appear to mind being on the bottom, but then they're high half the time. *The one exception is when a stoner plays a sport. That moves them up to the secondary consumer tier: snakes.

Adults in your life will tell you it's always been this way. They lived through it and we will too. Basically, suck it up, Sparky. Supposedly this social jungle disappears after high school. That was my light at the end of the four-year-long hallway, but I wasn't holding my breath.

See why getting off campus for bowling was nice? Maybe you love school. Maybe you're a beautiful lion and can't wait to stalk the halls. I'm not an introvert, but I'd been in the spotlight (not in a good way) as gossip swirled around me in my last school.

I'd been chum.

I had two words about my experience: Never. Again.

So bowling was my place to burrow and hide. Bowling had

given me precious time with my grandma I would always treasure. Bowling had saved me last year when my family fell apart. It gave me a reason to get out of the house and helped me block out some of the ugliness—at least for a few hours. If my plan worked, bowling would be my ticket out of here.

The bell rang and I took my time grabbing my bowling ball and shoes. By the time I got on the activity bus it was almost full. I liked to get on the bus last so I didn't have to sit awkwardly by myself for ten minutes waiting for the bus to load. I slid into my regular seat, the one right behind the driver's seat, placing my bowling ball bag between my feet so it wouldn't slide around once the bus got moving.

"Hello, Ali," the bus driver said. "Have a good summer?"

"Hey, Mrs. Mathews." Stop. Don't even say it. Because, yes, other kids had been kind enough to inform me how nerdy-weird-uncool it was to be friends with the bus driver. Whatever. Our eyes met in the rectangular mirror over the front window and I had the urge to blurt out that it had been the worst summer of my life. "It was okay. You?"

"Wonderful. I slept in every morning and enjoyed visits from my grandkids."

"Nice," I said.

Outside my window the last stragglers—probably the ones who slapped the snooze button too many times—wound through the cars and into the building. The noise level on the bus sounded like the inside of a busy bee hive.

Mrs. M fired up the bus and the floor rumbled under my feet as Coach Looper, the gym teacher and wrestling coach, jumped aboard. He held onto the silver pole and called roll from his clipboard.

I stared down at my unpainted fingernails while I half-listened for my name.

"Ali Frost?"

"Here."

"Paige Smith?"

"Here!" Her voice came from the back of the bus.

Oh, fun. Class with P3 all semester. And Paige never went anywhere without one of her side-kicks so that meant—

"Gwen Itzlrab?"

"Here, barely. Do they sell coffee at the bowling alley?"

"Not to students," Coach Looper said without looking up from the clipboard. "Dax DeLeon?"

DeLeon? My gaze flicked up to the overhead mirror and searched the faces. Yep, Dax DeLeon sat in the back row with the cool kids. A smirking Dax DeLeon as his laughing eyes met mine in the mirror. I pried my gaze away and back outside to the blur of live oak trees on the ten-minute drive to the alley.

So what? So, some of the annoying popular kids were in my class? I'd simply make sure to pick a lane far from them and do my thing. This was my time. My time to practice. My time to escape reality. I wouldn't let anyone mess that up.

The bus pulled up to the front entrance and Coach stood, tucking his clipboard under his arm. "Listen up. Head inside to the front counter for shoes. Once you've got those, proceed to a lane marked with a red cone. Pair up. That person will be your bowling partner for the semester."

I exited the bus first and hustled my behind to stake out my lane, nodding to Mr. Jones on my way past the shoe rental counter.

"You better have a teacher with you, Ali, or your ass is grass," he said.

"I do. And don't say 'ass' in front of me. I'm a young impressionable kid," I said without slowing down. I made it down to the farthest coned-off lane, dropped my backpack, and sat to change shoes. In the middle of tying my second shoe, a pair of sneakers entered my view.

I knew those sneakers.

"You can't sit here," I said, not even looking up.

24

"I can too," Dax said, doing exactly that, taking the chair next to me.

"No." I sat up like my back was attached to a spring. Because anywhere Dax was, Paige and crew were sure to follow.

"OMG, Frosty has her own bowling shoes!" Gwen squeaked.

"And her own bowling ball." Paige managed to make it sound pitiful.

Nope, nope, just no.

"All right, people," Coach said from down at lane number one. "Make sure you're with the partner you want because you'll be stuck—I mean, you'll be partnered—with them all semester."

"I'm not kidding, DeLeon. You need to take your fan club and leave." I stood and lifted my chin at him. "I've already got a partner."

Dax stood also, an imposing wall of football player. "Who?"

I darted my eyes down all the lanes and back. I found my white knight two lanes over. "Nolan! Nolan Baker's my partner. Right, Nolan?"

"No. Get lost, Frosty."

"Thanks a lot, Nolan." Dang it. I forgot he hated me ever since I'd ruined our electricity project in physical science last year. And accidentally shocked him. Sure. I guess five milliamps will stay in your memory for a while. Especially because we got a "D" on the project and Nolan had a bald spot on his scalp for a few months.

Nolan smiled at Paige. "But Paige can be my partner."

"Are you joking?" Paige wrinkled her nose. "I mean, bless your heart."

"Yeah. As if, Baker," Gwen said.

"I'll be your partner, Dax," Paige said, sidling up to him. They looked good together. Like a matched set. The cheerleader and the quarterback. Barbie and Ken. Sandy and Danny.

Dax took a casual step away from Paige which put him right next to me. "No thanks."

"Smith and Itzlrab. Frost and DeLeon." Coach scribbled down the teams, setting them in stone for the semester. "No partner, Baker? You'll be with me. Now let's all have fun."

It was a toss-up as to who was the most peeved: Nolan, Paige, or me.

Paige pouted, Nolan shot me a glare (how was his having to bowl with Coach my fault?), and I turned my annoyance toward Dax.

"What are you doing, DeLeon?"

"Picking a partner like everyone else."

"There are twenty other kids here—some of them are even on the football team."

"True. But none of them have their own bowling ball."

"So?"

"So, I'm a competitive guy. I figure you must be pretty good to have your own ball."

"I could just be a weirdo who likes to carry a bowling ball around."

"Are you?"

"If I say yes, will you go find another partner?"

"Nope."

I narrowed my eyes at him and all he did was grin. Fine. Whatever. I stood, keeping the ball return between us and laid down the rules. "If you took this class as a blow-off then go find another partner, because I'm dead serious about this class. No goofing off, no wasting time, and absolutely no gossiping on this lane. I don't have the time or patience for that. Got it?"

"Uh huh." Dax moved until he was in my space with only the ball return separating us. "Can I ask you something?"

"No."

"What did I ever do to you? Because most people like me."

"Congratulations. Do you mind if we stop talking about you and bowl now?"

"Well, I can see why you don't have any friends."

"You know nothing about me." He didn't know I didn't have friends. I mean, I didn't but that was a personal choice.

"I do. I know about you."

"Like what?"

"Like you're in Dr. Boyd's office enough that the secretary knows you and you give Kevin Twinkies at lunch. Also, you have a unique way of dressing."

"Those are observations. Not knowing, but good try."

"That's the point. I'm trying to be friendly here. Everyone needs friends."

"I don't." I picked up a ten-pound bowling ball and slammed it lightly into his stomach. "Now bowl."

5

ARE YOU STALKING ME?

Dax

Student Parking Lot, 3:20 p.m.

I was heading to the parking lot after school to grab my football gear when I spied with my watchful eye my new bowling partner shoving stuff into the trunk of a vintage Volvo. If you'd have asked me to pick Ali's car out of this full parking lot, I'd have guessed correctly. Before you get upset thinking I'm making some derogatory comment about Ali Frost—settle down. Totally the opposite. That Volvo was unique—just like Ali. A lot of kids I knew wouldn't be caught dead in a beater car like Ali's. I liked that about her.

Considering how much I'd annoyed her in first period, I shouldn't bug her again. Not until next bowling class anyway. Yet...

"Hey, partner!" I called, lengthening my stride in her direction.

She slammed her trunk closed before turning to look at me with a sad, pitiful head shake. By the time I arrived next to her car, she'd already buckled in and started her ignition. It sure looked like she was in a hurry to avoid me the way she threw her car into gear, gripped the steering wheel with two hands, and began to pull forward through the empty parking space in front of her.

Oh, whoa. I did a double take on the pavement.

"Stop!" Jumping forward, I tapped the hood of her car twice.

She stopped so abruptly her car rocked. She stabbed me with a narrow-eyed gaze before lowering her window. "DeLeon. You are seriously—"

"Hold that thought." I walked in front of her car and picked up the guitar case she came within a foot of crushing. Lifting it a little higher and giving it a wiggle, I grinned at her before turning to the group of guys three car spaces over. "Grady! One day someone's going to run your guitar over."

"Whoever does will have to deal with me." He came over and grabbed it from me. "This Fender is irreplaceable."

I walked around next to Ali again, resting one hand on the roof of her car. "You're welcome."

"For what?"

"I saved you from running over Grady's guitar."

"You want me to thank you for that? It's not my guitar. I'm also not the genius who put a black guitar case on the black pavement and left it unsupervised."

She was absolutely right about that.

"We keep running into each other." I grinned. "Twice in one day. It almost feels like you're stalking me."

"Stalking you?" She raised one eyebrow at me. "I'm sorry, who just sprinted across the parking lot to talk to me? Who was it who switched into my bowling class after sneaking a look at my schedule? It's like you can't quit me."

"Maybe I can't," I said, mouth quirked into a small smile.

The sun brought to life yellow streaks in her light green

eyes. Gorgeous eyes. So gorgeous my thoughts scattered and I stood dazed, like I'd taken a hit to my helmet.

"Dax! What are you doing? You're going be late for practice."

Right. I waved to TJ who'd called from two rows over where he was grabbing out his football equipment from the bed of his Takoma. "Be right there!"

"If you're late and coach makes us do extra up-downs, I'll spit on your lunch for a week."

He wouldn't. I knew he was bluffing, mostly because he couldn't spit worth a darn and he'd end up dribbling it down his shirt.

"Oh, gross," Ali said. "You should go."

"I'm going." I winked at her which normally had girls blushing. Not Ali.

"You did *not* just wink at me."

"I did. I winked." I grinned at Ali's reaction. "Guilty as charged."

"Take it back," she demanded.

"I would, but I can't. Winks are nonreturnable. But I'll tell you what… You can wink at me and then we'll be even."

"Aaargh. I can't even with you." She huffed out a breath, gripped the steering wheel so tightly her knuckles turned white, and sent me a look that loosely translated into "You're an idiot."

"See you in class, partner." And you know what I did? Yep. I winked at her again.

Ali sent me one last narrow-eyed look and drove off. I felt sure she'd be thinking of me. Maybe not nice thoughts, but she would be thinking of me.

I grabbed my gear and hustled inside because I did not want to be the reason the team did extra drills. I'd have a whole lot of pissed off teammates. Not good for a quarterback who needed his teammates to come through with a big season. Coach Devlin said we needed to up our game every week in case collegiate scouts were in the stands.

I was counting on football to outweigh my average GPA and help me get into college. When I was young, I had the attention span of a gnat but the energy of a hummingbird. Constantly on the go. So, my parents signed me up for sports back in first grade to help burn off all that excess energy. It clicked with me and had grown to be as much a part of my life as eating and breathing. Being an athlete was who I was. I'd been working hard at becoming a better player every year. Eating healthy, extra workouts, hitting up the most challenging summer football and lacrosse camps every summer.

The next two hours I threw myself into practice. Drills, practicing the snap with our freshman center—working on the snap count—and a few rounds of fake hand-offs before focusing on pass plays with the receivers.

"Dax, you've got to pick up your receivers quicker to make that play work!" Coach yelled from the sidelines. "TJ, obviously you've got the speed but you're overrunning your mark and making it harder on your QB. Let's try a few slant routes."

Near the end of practice my concentration took a hit when my dad's car pulled into the parking lot. No doubt my dad was my biggest fan. He talked all the time about me following in his footsteps and playing for his alma mater. We both did, only I wasn't sure I could pull that off. Some days I stood on the field feeling like an imposter. Like someone was going to point out that I was doing it all wrong and then everyone would see I didn't have the talent everyone had raved about.

I overthrew the pass. And the next one and the one after that. Dammit. I had to get out of my head and focus on what I was doing on the practice field.

"Water break!" Coach called. "Everyone hydrate and hit the weight room."

I pulled off my helmet, wiped the sweat off my face with my practice jersey, and grabbed a water bottle as Coach walked up to me. "I know what you're going to say, Coach. Get out of my own way."

"You're good, Dax. You've got natural instincts—a feel for the game on where to go with the ball—but you've got to trust yourself. In that split second when you doubt yourself you give the opposition an opening to attack. Doubt leads you to press too hard and then you're over your head. You're in—"

"Quicksand." That was the reason we'd almost lost in the playoffs last year. I second guessed myself on one throw. My hesitation caused an interception. Luckily their defense got called for holding and our team went on to win and we'd made it into the championship game. Except I did the same thing in the final game only we weren't lucky. We lost.

"Exactly. Mental quicksand." Coach Devlin lightly tapped his clipboard on my shoulder. "Stop overthinking and trust your instincts. Get out of your head."

"I'm trying, Coach." Football was my future. My ticket to college. My dream since I put on my first shoulder pads. So, yeah, I worked hard to win. I hated losing almost more than anything. It was one thing to get outplayed, but causing my own downfall... That was hard to swallow.

"Depressurize. Stop worrying about scouts. And"—his gaze moved up the hill to where my dad sat in the parking lot watching and over to the cheerleaders practicing on the track before landing back on me—"get rid of distractions. Not even some cute cheerleader watching you from the sidelines."

"Working on it." That was one of the reasons—although not the main one—why I'd broken up with Paige at the beginning of summer. No way was I going to let my teammates down again.

"Maybe it'll help to remember it's just a game," Coach said.

"Just a game." I could still see the interception I'd thrown in the championship game. The one that cost us the title. The despondent faces of my teammates when I'd let them down. Could still feel the clap of pity from Coach on my shoulder and hear the muted frustration in the locker room. "Right. I'll try, Coach."

"Head to the trainer and have her work on that shoulder." He gave me a pointed look before heading off the field.

I hadn't told a soul that my shoulder wasn't one-hundred percent after last season's injury. There was no way I wanted the team to worry. Or worse, let doubt creep through our ranks and destroy our motivation. Figures Coach picked up on it.

I jogged to the sidelines, stripping off my practice jersey and pads on the way. Grabbing up my bag, I walked over to where TJ waited for me.

"Everything okay?" he asked as we headed in, the last two stragglers on the team.

"Absolutely." Power of positive thinking, right? I *would* lead our team to the state championship again this year. Only this year we were going to win. I wasn't letting anything take my focus off that goal. Not my shoulder. Not a girlfriend. Not—

"Hey, Dax." Paige had planted herself in the middle of the sidewalk. "The rest of the girls already left for Scoops. I told them I'd catch a ride with you when you're ready."

"Sorry. I'm not going to Scoops today." Or any day soon. Sure, I'd miss the post-practice milkshake, but I had to put an end to Paige fluttering around me like we were still a couple.

"Oh." She blinked up at me and I couldn't tell if she was shocked that I'd turned her down or waiting for me to change my mind.

"Maybe TJ can give you a ride," I offered. Best friends took a bullet for each other, right?

"No," TJ said. "I'm not going either."

"I'll catch a ride with Luke then," Paige said. Luke, the guy I'd been jealous of last year.

"Have fun," I said and walked onto the grass to get around her and into the building.

TJ shook his head. "Has any guy ever ended things with

Paige? Because she's like a pilot fish on a shark. Maybe you need to tell her again."

"I couldn't have said it any plainer. Not without being a jerk."

"Time to be a jerk then."

"Nah, I think I've got another way figured out."

6

I'M OKAY–YOU'RE OKAY

Ali

Breakfast with Dad, Oct 16, 7:28 a.m.

"One more week down." I sat on the side of my bed recording into my phone for my vlog. "Anxiety level: seven. DeLeon stresses me out. Who does Dax DeLeon think he is? He's too cocky by far. If I had a way to knock that cheeky, arrogant, swaggering smirk off his face, I'd do it."

I cocked my head, listening to the drone of Dad's music slithering down the hall from the kitchen and shook my head into the camera.

"I used to like mornings in my house. I can't believe I'm saying this, but I miss Dad's classic rock. Ever since mom left it's been German opera 24/7. Have you listened to German opera? It can be dark and depressing. I'm talking pain, death, and rats scurrying through shadowy alleys depressing. Nothing starts off a day like Requiem for a Divorced Dad. Positive affirmation: I breathe in calmness and breathe out nervousness."

I was already dressed for school: a bowling tournament T-shirt and old sweat pants I'd cut off at the knees. I made an attempt to control my frizzy curls by scrunching my hair into a messy knot with an elastic. Of course, I couldn't find my flip-flops—thanks to my Golden Retriever, Bella, and her shoe obsession—so I shoved my feet into my Vans and made my way downstairs to the kitchen.

I sucked in one deep breath before I threw myself into the room and went through my "it's a great day to be alive" routine.

Dad stood at the stove mechanically pushing eggs around in a cast iron skillet. The familiar scent of burned toast floated in the air.

"Morning, Dad!" I flashed him the smile he needed—the one that assured him that he hadn't messed me up with his solo parenting the last year.

"Hey, Ali-Cat." He flashed me the smile I needed—the one that assured me that he wasn't a totally broken man since my mom, his wife of twenty years, left him after a hot torrid affair with the assistant football coach of the high school they'd both worked at. The high school I used to attend. The high school that spread the juicy gossip about the complete, horrific collapse of our lives.

We had a morning routine we'd fallen into. Dad cooked some barely edible breakfast which I made a half-hearted effort to eat. While Dad dished the eggs onto plates, I scraped the burned surface of toast into the trash before spreading the butter and red raspberry jam. Coffee for him. Juice for me. Then we'd sit at the counter and each fake how okay we were. Was it healthy? No, but it's what had gotten us both this far, so...

"How are your classes? Everything okay?" he asked.

"Good. Really good." I forked up some eggs, burned bits and all.

His gaze scoured my face. "Are you sure? Because—"

"Seriously, I'm having a great year." The lie slid out easily. Great was relative anyway.

"Good." Dad's shoulders relaxed and the lines across his forehead smoothed out. "Are you making new friends this year?"

"It's only second semester." I ripped off a piece of toast and crammed it in my mouth to avoid having to talk. The less I said the better. Dad had enough on his plate.

"Ali..." He put his coffee down, so I knew he was about to get serious. Which meant he'd reach into his limited bag of "dad tricks" and pull out his most powerful weapon—his sad, somber dad eyes.

"I'm running late." I jerked my face away to avoid his gaze. Sliding from the stool, I scraped my uneaten eggs into Bella's bowl and dropped my plate in the sink. I usually caved under his dad eyes. Not today. I loved my dad but I also had a solid plan to get through my last year of high school.

"You can't isolate yourself, Ali," he said. "It's not healthy."

"Then why are you?" I took three steps until I stood directly opposite him at the island. He wore jeans and a polo shirt with "Coach Frost" embroidered over his heart. "Haven't you been hiding out here in the house playing Mr. Mom ever since you quit your job last year?"

"That's different." He wrapped both hands around his mug of coffee. "Your world was turned upside down. You need stability."

"It was a year ago. I'm moving forward," I said. "But you look awfully stuck. Do you even leave the house when I'm at school? And going to the grocery store doesn't count."

"Of course I do." His eyes avoided mine. "I go to the gym."

"And...?" My father blinked a few times before dragging his gaze to meet mine and he might as well have reached his hand into my chest and yanked out my heart. Except he couldn't because my mother had gotten to that vital organ first. My dad's eyes said so much. Much more than he'd admit to me. They said he was still in pain. Still devastated. They said he was lost.

37

"I need to make sure you're okay," he said.

And I needed to make sure he was okay before I went away to college.

"You need to get out of the house, Dad. You need to get back to work. The high school wants you back. They've been calling since last year."

He shook his head. "Would you want to go back there?"

Absolutely not. "Fair point. What about one of the other schools? At least three other schools have left messages. It's time, Dad. You've got to let it go and get your life back."

"Probably. I don't know." Dad ran a hand around the back of his neck and released a long sigh before tilting his head and giving me a long look. "Okay. I'll try... As soon as I know you're okay."

"I'm okay. Great even." I plastered on a smile. "I'm making friends. Ogling cute boys. Skipping class. You know, all the normal stuff."

"Skipping class?" Dad shot me a dark frown.

"Kidding! See? I even have my sense of humor back," I said. "I told you I was fine."

"I'll believe it when I see it, kiddo."

See it? My dad had become a helicopter parent. Unbelievable.

* * *

I had a love-hate relationship with bowling class. I loved that I got to practice my bowling. I loved being in the bowling alley. There was something about the repetitive sound of pins crashing in the cavernous space that relaxed me. It soothed me. All the noise blended together into the background allowing me to focus on my form. Usually.

I hated having to listen to Paige and Gwen's litany of the

newest gossip, endless attempts to flirt with Dax, and high-pitched giggles that drilled their way into my consciousness. I hated that Dax was either looking at my butt (sort of not his fault since he had to sit behind me waiting for his turn) or trying to talk to me.

The first week of class I'd ignored him but the guy was nothing if not persistent. Ignoring wasn't working. So this week I'd apply a new tactic. Maybe if I responded he'd feel like he won the "annoy the geek girl" game and he'd stop.

I'd just finished putting on my bowling shoes and setting my sneakers to the side when Dax joined me at our assigned lane, sitting next to me.

"Morning, Ali." He smiled at me, those dark gorgeous eyes of his snagged mine.

"Morning, De—Dax." See? I could be nice. I could play his game until he got bored and moved on.

His eyebrows shot up at my response. "You're talking to me? I mean, of course you are. We're bowling partners. Maybe— eventually—more than that. I feel like this is the beginning of a beautiful—"

"Whoa, there. Let's not go overboard. How about we bowl? You're up first."

He pointed at me with a bad boy grin so cute it was easy to see why girls went crazy over him. "Okay. But you might as well go first while I put my shoes on."

"Sure." I retrieved my ball from its bag and held my right hand over the air vent to make sure it was dry.

"Morning, Dax," Paige sing-songed. Yep. Paige and Gwen had arrived, settling in at the lane next to us, late and loud.

"Hey," he said with barely a glance over at his ex.

Moving onto the approach, I gripped my ball.

"That is one sweet ball," Dax said.

I jerked my head around to see if he was being sarcastic, but no, he was serious. Today I was breaking in my new 900 Global

Boo-Yah! ball. I figured he wouldn't be interested in its low differential, high RG core. "Thanks."

My plan for bowling class was to use my time to strengthen the weak areas of my game. Up first: converting spares. I'd been missing too many 7 pin spares lately. I didn't need strikes today. My goal was to convert the 7 pin ten times in a row. I set my body, lifted my ball, found my target, and threw.

"You're hooking left," Dax said.

"That's the plan," I said, my gaze tracking my ball, mentally coaxing it along as it flew down the lane and took out the 7 pin.

"Frosty missed half the pins!" Gwen squealed with excitement.

"Aw, too bad, Frosty," Paige said. "I guess your own bowling shoes and bowling ball can only do so much. Too bad, so sad."

Dax threw a look over at Gwen and Paige. "You do know she did that on—"

"I'm sure you'll get a strike next time." Gwen snickered.

"You should watch Dax. You might learn something." Paige fluttered her eyelashes at him. "Dax is an excellent bowler. He always beats me on our bowling dates."

Dax mumbled something under his breath as he stood for his turn.

"Used to beat you," he ground out through clenched teeth. "We haven't been together for months."

"Every couple takes a break now and then." Paige shook her blond hair, confidence oozing from every hair follicle.

His gaze moved from Paige to me and his frown disappeared sliding into a slow, flirtatious smile. A smile aimed at me.

"Not a break. I'm with someone else now." His eyes burned me up, hot and intense. "Right, Ali?"

"Wh—what?" My gaze darted over to Paige and Gwen's dumbfounded faces and then back to Dax.

"I know you wanted to keep it a secret, but that's impossible, babe." He winked at me.

"Are you kidding me?" Paige said, her voice pitching high. "You're joking. I don't believe it."

If I was reading this right...Dax DeLeon wanted me to be his pretend girlfriend to fend off his ex. Why would I do that? I didn't want or need any of these people in my life. In fact, it was the last thing I wanted.

Although... *Make friends. Ogle cute guys. I'll believe it when I see it, kiddo.*

"Believe it. Ali and I are..." He raised an eyebrow at me and waited. He was giving me the option to go along with him or deny it. "Ali?"

7

YOU DIDN'T EVEN KNOW HER NAME

Dax

The idea to use Ali to get Paige off my back and accept we were done came to me last week. It was a brilliant idea. The only thing was I hadn't planned on putting it into motion this soon. I figured after a few weeks of being bowling partners we'd get to know each other. Become friends. Then I'd ask her.

Unfortunately, I'd let Paige's continued pushing—acting like we were still together—mess up my game plan. I let her draw me offside. So I tossed up a Hail Mary pass and hoped Ali would catch it. Based on the cool narrow-eyed gaze Ali had pinned on me, she was going to stay on the sidelines. Maybe even call a foul. It was too soon. She didn't know me. Heck, she didn't even like me. Why would she help me?

I nodded at her. Fair enough. "Yeah, I'm k—"

"It's true," Ali said. She shrugged and gestured with her hand between us. "We're a…thing."

Gwen gasped.

Paige snorted in disbelief. "You didn't even know her name last week!"

"That didn't stop him." Ali sent me a half-smile, but her eyes sparked with humor. "He fell for me the minute he saw me. The second time he saw me he begged me to go out with him. I didn't really like him at first, but I felt sorry for him. It was pretty pathetic, so I agreed to a pity-date with him. It wasn't half bad, so now we're a thing."

Oh, nice. She'd help me but she was going to make me pay for it. Two could play at that game.

"There's no way." Paige parked her hands on her hips. "The two of you? It makes no sense."

"Tell us about it. It's that jock-nerd thing. Isn't that right, stud?"

"That's right, gummy bear." I swallowed a laugh. This would be a fun semester.

"OMG! Nicknames? You're at the nickname stage already?" Gwen grabbed Paige's arm. "Did you and Dax get to the nickname stage?"

That would be a no.

Paige didn't respond. She stood blinking at me in surprise before whispering, "Gummy bear?"

"Because I'm sweet, soft-hearted, and huggable." Ali nodded and poked me in the arm. "Can we get back to bowling now? My spare conversion isn't going to fix itself. Your turn, boo."

Paige glared at Ali before turning her over-bright eyes on me.

"I know what this is. You're trying to make me jealous. That's all. You'll get bored." She flicked a dismissive gaze over to Ali. "I'll wait."

"I'm not trying to make you jealous." Another reason why I'd broken up with Paige: in Paige's world, everything revolved around her.

"Whatever." She pinned on a fake smile and smoothed her hair. After one last narrowed-eyed glance at Ali she snapped, "Gwen. Bathroom. Now."

The two girls stomped off, whispering madly the whole way. Ali sat biting her bottom lip as she tracked their exit.

"Well that was fun," I said, trying to get things back to normal. Although Ali and I didn't have a normal. Yet.

She only frowned, her attention still focused on the bathroom.

"Thanks for playing along." I slid over onto the seat next to her. "I thought for sure you were going to say no."

Her gaze slid to mine and away. "I almost did."

"Well, thanks. I owe you one."

"Yeah you do," she said. "I aim to collect."

"We should talk about how to work this…"

"Later, okay?" She sighed. "I've already lost too much practice time on you and your fan club."

"Right." Grabbing a ball from the rack, I moved to the lane, set my sights on the pins, and rolled. It wasn't even close to a strike.

"Bummer. The Big Four," Ali said.

"Excuse me?"

She nodded down to the pins. "The Big Four. When you leave the 4-6-7-10 pins. It's a tough shot."

Paige and Gwen returned to the lane next to us. I shut out their whispers and sharp glances and focused on bowling. That's what Ali wanted and I owed her. I stepped up for my attempted spare, aiming for the 4 pin and throwing hard in hopes the pin I hit would take out the other three with it. I managed to knock down two pins.

Ali picked up her ball and took her position to roll. She had a smooth, confident delivery. Once again, she didn't get a strike but turned to grab her ball with a satisfied smile on her face.

"Why are you aiming to the left?" I'd watched her bowl all last week and most of the time she rolled strikes.

"Practicing picking up spares."

"Oh. You're really good at bowling." My friends and I bowled sometimes, but none of us knew anything about bowling. "I guess you bowl a lot?"

Gwen laughed and jumped into our conversation. "The old guy at the shoe counter knows her. Said she's here all the time. That she practically lives here on weekends."

"Aw. It's sad not to have any friends," Paige said. "You're stuck bowling all by yourself every Friday and Saturday night."

Reason number three I'd broken up with Paige: She could be mean.

"Not anymore." I sent Ali a smile. "Right, Ali?"

"Sure," Ali said. "But the reason I bowl a lot is because I'm on the bowling team at school. So, save your pity."

"We have a bowling team?" Gwen asked before breaking into giggles.

That was a surprise to me too. It must have shown on my face because Ali arched an eyebrow in my direction.

"And, Gwen?" Ali waited until Gwen stopped laughing. "The 'old guy' at the counter is a Vietnam veteran and a two-time PBA champion. His name is Mr. Jones."

"Like I care. Ugh. I broke a nail!" Gwen dropped her ball loudly back to the return and held up her hand for everyone to see. "I just got them done yesterday."

Ali regarded Gwen like she was a gutter ball in a tense game. The two girls couldn't be more different, so yeah.

With a shake of her head, Ali turned her back on the other lane. "You're up."

I wasn't the excellent bowler Paige made me out to be but I was competitive. I liked to excel and I loved to win. Which meant this was the perfect opportunity.

"Do you mind helping me with my technique?" I asked.

Ali blinked at me twice. "Sure. First of all, instead of aiming down at the pins, target the floorboards."

That piece of advice improved my roll instantly. Enough that I might even beat TJ and Grady next time we played.

"Is the team ready for Sterling this Friday, Dax?" Paige asked, right in the middle of my roll.

I kept my focus and threw my ball—a strike—before responding.

"We're ready." Sterling didn't have a strong football program so this should be an easy win. Should be. I had to admit with the way I'd been off my game, I didn't count on sure things lately.

"We've got a new cheer for it," Paige said. "I think you're going to love it."

I doubted I'd even hear it. We came out of the locker room so hyper-focused that not much off the field registered.

"It's super awesome," Gwen said. "Paige does an aerial and lands in a split."

"I'm happy to continue our tradition of the good luck kiss before the game." Paige smiled like we had a secret between us.

"Not necessary." Or wanted. I knew what Paige was doing. Acting like we were still together while getting in a dig at Ali. It didn't look like Ali minded, but I did. "To be honest, I don't actually believe in luck."

"I guess you'll be going to the game now?" Gwen asked Ali, only to have Paige elbow her in the ribs. "Or not. That's right. You bowling nerds never go to the football games."

Ali looked across at Gwen. "We bowling nerds do whatever we want. We're sheep dogs, not sheep."

"OMG, she totally called herself a dog!" Gwen laughed.

"So, you're not going to Dax's game?" Paige crossed her arms, looking all superior. "What kind of supportive girlfriend are you?"

"The kind who has her own life. The kind who doesn't wrap herself around her guy like a boa constrictor and choke the life out of him. The kind who can be supportive without attaching herself to him like a burr on a bear's butt."

I tried not to laugh. I failed.

8

IT AIN'T ALL RAINBOWS AND
UNICORN FARTS

Ali

VARSITY BOWLING PRACTICE, 3:46 P.M.

I used to be good at making friends. At least I thought so until my friends had turned on me. Them and every other kid at school. When my dad and the counselor suggested I transfer schools, I jumped on it. Dad felt horrible that I was being blamed for something that wasn't my fault. Heck, it wasn't even his fault but he felt responsible.

Whatever. New school. No wild gossip. No kids and ex-friends stuffing "You suck" and "Grow a pair" notes in my locker. And those were the nicer notes. No angry glances or "accidental" pushes from behind. My dad thought the transfer would help. A fresh start with new friends. I decided not having friends would help. Instead, I curled up in a protective shell like a three-banded armadillo and had been rolling quietly through the hallways of my new high school toward graduation.

Until this morning. Until this morning when the look on my dad's face broke me. My smart, driven, five-time Texas-high-school-state-champ winning football coach of a dad had been blindsided. Taken out. And it was like he was afraid to get back on the field. He needed to move on. My mother sure had. My dad deserved to be happy too. But he wouldn't until he stopped worrying about me.

That was why I'd gone along with Dax's wild story. When Dax told Paige he and I were together I was shocked and a little pissed. I opened my mouth to deny it—emphatically—but my dad's voice whispered in my head... *Making friends. Ogling cute boys. I'll believe it when I see it, kiddo.*

So, I said yes. I'd help DeLeon out and he could help me right back. Dax would be part of my show and tell to assure my dad he didn't have to worry about me. Ogling cute boys. Check.

Next up? Making friends. What did I have in common with Shaniqua Johnson, Gabriela Lopez, Mariko Takahashi, Rowena Clark, and Bhakti Patel? Other than we were all on the varsity girls' bowling team, I had no idea. Which was all my fault. Time to find out.

I pulled open the front door of Bowl-O-Rama and joined my teammates on the far side of the alley. Wait...not just teammates. Potential friends. Maybe.

Coach Diamond was already going over today's practice goals down on lane twelve when I slid into one of the seats.

Bhakti sent me a smile and small wave of her hand from across the lane.

"You're late, Frost," Coach D said. "That's a demerit. Two more and you've got BPD."

"Yes, Coach." BPD, aka ball polishing duty, sucked. Since not every girl on our team had her own bowling ball the school had five. Coach was fanatical about keeping the team's balls clean. No one liked having to stay late to clean them.

"All right. SWD time. We've only got two lanes today on account of that rug-rat birthday party down at the end, so don't waste time chattering." Coach D tucked her clipboard under one arm. "ISD in thirty minutes."

Coach was big on acronyms. Probably from her years in the Army. SWD. Stretching, warm-up on the lanes, and drills. ISD was individualized skill development. These weren't actual bowling acronyms. Coach made them up on the fly.

As we stood in a loose circle stretching our shoulders, backs, hips, and hands, I cleared my throat and made my move.

"So, anyone watching the new mini-series on PBS?" Lame, sure. I was a little rusty at girl talk and a lot guilty that I'd mostly kept to myself ever since I'd joined the team at the end of last season. But I had to start somewhere.

All the girls sort of paused and blinked at me in surprise. Which I totally got. But it only lasted a second.

"The one with Benedict Cumberbatch? Giiirrrl, yes." Shani fanned herself with her hand. "That man is fine."

"I can't believe they ended last week on that cliffhanger!" Bhakti said. "Don't forget we're watching at my house this weekend. Ali, you should come. Or join our group chat if you can't make it."

"Yes, Ali!" Gaby smiled at me.

Mari nodded. "It would be fun to have all of us there."

"Are you sure?" These girls had every right to reject me.

"Of course. Why wouldn't we be?" Rowena looked genuinely confused.

"It wasn't like you've been mean to us or anything," Mari said. "Unlike some of the stuck-up kids."

"Well, no, but I…" I flinched as heat rushed into my cheeks because I'd ignored their offer of friendship. Repeatedly. They'd been amazingly sweet and inclusive when I'd arrived toward the end of bowling season last year. I was the one who had kept them at arm's length, politely turning down every study session, pizza party, or movie-marathon invitation.

"Rejected us?" Shani prompted.

Right. I had. I hadn't meant to be a jerk. It had been a desperate attempt at self-preservation.

"A lot," Gaby added.

"I'm sorry." I forced myself to look at each girl. I needed to own what I'd done.

"We're pretty used to it," Rowena said.

"Everyone has some quirk. Heck, I'm forgetful. My mama says my brain is a colander." Shani worked her way around the group. "Ro's afraid of everything. Gaby's gullible."

I glanced over at Gabriela.

"It's true." She shrugged.

"Mari is fanatical about the environment—"

"We only have one planet." Mari's face went fierce.

"I'm indecisive." Bhakti frowned. "I think. Some days. I guess is all relative."

Rowena nodded. "Everyone's a weirdo in their own way."

"We figured you were anti-social."

"I guess I was. But I'm trying to change." I tensed, distrusting how easy they were making this. I wouldn't blame them one bit if they made me grovel first. Put me through some embarrassing payback. I totally deserved it. "Trying to be a better friend."

"Okay." Mari smiled at me.

"Okay?" *Okay?* That simple? I told you these girls were nice. Guilt poked at my belly since my wanting acceptance into their circle had an ulterior motive. Not that it would hurt them in any way, but I was planning on using them. Their friendship. "I mean, okay. Thanks."

"Now that we're friends..." Shani leaned forward, a big grin on her face. "Giiirrrl, what is up with you and Dax DeLeon?"

"Uh..." Dax and I had only gone public this morning in first period, but in high school time, that was ages ago. Gossip flew faster than a high-speed internet connection. Especially when it involved the star quarterback. Dax DeLeon could get away with almost anything, but maybe not this time. This time he was breaking all the social hierarchy rules by being involved with an unknown certified bowling nerd.

"What?" Bhakti's eyes went wide. "Ali and Dax?"

"We definitely need details," Gaby said.

"Truth." Rowena nodded. "Give it up. We're going to need all the dirty details."

"There's not much to tell," I said with a shrug which elicited frustrated groans from them all.

"Ladies!" Coach called her warning from the snack bar.

"Come on, Ali. We've never had front row seats to the cool kids before," Bhakti said. "We're usually in the top row of the bleacher seats."

"Yeah." Gaby nodded. "You can't hold out on us."

"I'm not. Honestly, there's nothing to tell." Their smiles and excitement disappeared quickly like when the team needed a strike but got a gutter-ball instead. Oh, man, I didn't want to let these girls down already. *"Yet.* There's nothing to tell yet. This thing between me and DeLeon—Dax—is brand new. And sort of sudden. He didn't even know I existed until last week."

That brightened their faces right back up.

"Wow." Mari sighed. "Like love at first sight."

"Hot jock falls for nerdy girl," Gaby said. "It's rom-com movie romantic."

"Whoa, there, Gaby." Shani held up her hand like a traffic cop. "It ain't all roses and unicorn farts. You need to watch your back, Ali. You know how I heard about it? Gwen was spilling it to all the cheerleaders in the girl's locker room. She said Paige is pissed. Really pissed. So be ready is all I'm saying."

This wasn't a surprise. I knew Paige was shocked when Dax first opened his mouth. When I went along and said it was true, her shock morphed, sliding right through pissed and ratcheting up to furious. Her face had pinched up, turned red, and her eyes narrowed on me like a wolverine eyes a defenseless rabbit. Paige and her friends could make a meal of me. I wasn't sure I was ready to handle that again. But I didn't have a choice. My dad came first; I needed to take care of my dad.

"Don't look so worried," Mari said. "You've got us now. We've got your back."

"Exactly," Bhakti agreed. "That's what friends do."

That hadn't been my experience, but I was sure they meant well. I didn't need anyone to have my back. I'd gone it alone before. Sort of, but I was stronger now. Okay, maybe not stronger, but smarter. I knew to watch my back. I wasn't as trusting or naïve this time. It might be painful and embarrassing, but I only had to last three more semesters and then I could escape this small town.

"All right, ladies! ISD time!" Translation: Individual skills development. This was the time we each worked on our weak areas. Coach D wiped the last of the Cheetos dust from her lips, tossed the napkin in the trash, and moved to the first lane. "We've got our first meet in a few weeks against Hawthorne."

During practice, Coach spent a few minutes stressing the fun aspect of bowling. But she was competitive. She brought up her favorite barracuda/goldfish analogy but didn't bust out the whole speech. My guess was she was saving it for later in the season.

Her take-no-prisoners attitude was an uncomfortable fit for a team of awkward nerds who'd survived by surrendering at the slightest confrontation. Not that we didn't want to tap into our inner barracudas. We did. But it was a work in progress and we were still goldfish.

We sat while Shani and Gaby went first. Shani stepped onto the approach and settled into her stance.

I thought over the conversation with my teammates—no... my friends—and snickered. "Roses and unicorn farts. Unicorn farts, Shani?"

Sadly, this broke Shani's concentration mid-swing and her ball fell onto the lane with a crash.

"Johnson!" Coach chastised from four lanes over where she'd talked herself into a piece of the birthday girl's pink princess cake from the birthday girl's mom.

"It slipped, Coach," Shani called over.

"I'm sorry! It's just"—I laughed—"I mean, unicorn farts. What do they even smell like?"

"Like salt water taffy and sugar cookies had a baby, and the baby was dipped in a Cook-Out double chocolate milkshake. With whip cream. Everyone knows that."

We busted out laughing.

"What the tarnation is up with you girls today?" Coach said from behind us. "Frost, you know better than to interrupt a bowler's swing. You just got yourself another demerit."

"Sorry, Coach." But I wasn't really. That laugh—this new feeling of closeness with these girls—was worth another demerit. When everything went down last year, I'd escaped inside myself. Protected myself from the mess my mom made of our lives. From my dad's pain. From my pain. From the anger of kids at school. I'd locked up my heart, leaving it flash-frozen behind a wall of ice. Today was like a soft ray of sun shining down and melting it just a little.

After skills, we moved into knowledge building and then practicing what we'd learned. Then fun time (a quick game of around the world), psych time (today, Coach had us visualize our perfect roll), and we wrapped up with our five-minute closing meeting and a team cheer.

"Is everyone keeping up with their fitness workouts? Run, swim, or lift weights. I don't care as long as you're doing one of those." Coach gave us her IGMEOY ("I've got my eye on you") look. "Our first competition is just over two weeks away. We need a volunteer to host the first team pizza party that week. Any takers?"

This was the perfect opportunity for my dad to see I was

making friends. See that I was fine and he could stop worrying about me and focus on himself.

"Me." I raised my hand. "I will."

"Thank you, Frost." Coach penciled it onto her clipboard. "Make sure you send out the date, time, and address to the team."

"Niiice," Shani said.

Gaby winked at me, Mari smiled, Rowena nudged me with her shoulder, and Bhakti gave me a thumbs up.

Making new friends? Check.

9

BOWLING BOYFRIENDS ARE NOT A THING

Dax

ALI'S LOCKER, OCT 17, 7:51 A.M.

"Hey, babe." I leaned my shoulder against the locker next to Ali's and gave a gentle tug to her ponytail. "Good morning."

She turned her head toward me and pinned me with a sharp look. "What are you doing here?"

"Meeting my girl at her locker before school." I watched her face, amused at the slight grimace the words "my girl" elicited. Ali Frost was seemingly unimpressed with my quarterback status and I liked that. A lot. "It's 'B' day so we won't see each other in bowling today. Thought I'd, you know, catch you now. Walk you to class."

"Oh, right. The couple thing," she said, sliding her calculus book into her locker and slamming it closed. Calculus, huh? My pretend girlfriend was a brain. She turned to face me, leaning her shoulder against her locker with a foot of space between us. "First thing, don't call me babe. Just no. Second, are we really one of those couples? I feel sure we're one of those more modern couples who isn't joined at the hip."

I smiled down at her. "Normally, I would agree. Don't like those clingy couples myself." I'd been trying to extricate myself from that exact thing for months now. "But...the whole point of this is for Paige to see that you and I are together. So she'll move on and leave me alone."

"Fine. What else will this entail then?"

"Meet each other at our lockers a couple times a day."

"A couple times? As a boyfriend, you sure are high maintenance." She pushed away from the locker and started walking toward the science classrooms. I had to move fast to keep up with her.

"No, I'm not. Because as a couple, you're happy to see my face."

"Right. Fair warning, I can drum up sort of happy. But I doubt I can fake ecstatically happy like some of the girls around school. You do have quite a fan club."

"That's not really about me." I shrugged and dodged a trash can sitting in the center of the hallway. "It's about being the quarterback."

She arched an eyebrow at me.

"I'm not kidding. Anyway, we also need to eat lunch together, maybe hold hands once or twice, and the thing that should clinch it—you'll have to come by at the end of football practice to watch and wait for me."

Ali stopped on a dime and faced me. "Excuse me? Why?"

"Because all the girlfriends do." She tilted her head and sucked in a breath. I figured she was trying not to tell me to shove it. I pressed my lips together, holding back a smile. Man, how had I not seen this girl around school all this time?

"No. That doesn't even sound right."

"What's not right?"

"Why do I have to go to your practice?" She lifted her chin at me. "Why don't you come by the end of my bowling practice?"

"Bowling boyfriends? Yeah, that's not a thing."

"You've got me there. But we could be outliers. Trendsetters even. You can come watch me bowl and wait for me."

"Don't think I wouldn't. In fact, I enjoy watching you roll in bowling class." I grinned. "I enjoy it a lot. But it won't work."

"Are you always this negative?" she asked.

"Not negative. Practical. If you don't show up at the end of football practice, Paige and her friends aren't going to believe it. No one will. It's proof of life for our relationship. Hey, I don't write these rules. It's just how it works."

"Fine. But I protest the patriarchy."

"Patriarchy? No one told girls they had to stand on the sidelines ogling our six-packs."

"Except you just did. Just now."

"Right. But you have to admit that's a thing couples around here do. At least with football players."

"I guess. But that doesn't mean I have to like it."

"Understood. Maybe we guys don't like being used for sexual objectification. Ever think of that?"

"Nope."

I grinned, digging the fact that she didn't seem at all impressed with my jock status. I'd admit having girls look at me like I was some football god was a head trip when I was a freshman and a sophomore—but that got old. "As much as I'd like to ogle your bowling form for equality, football practice runs longer, so…"

"Okay. Lockers, lunch, and lusty eyes at the end of football practice. I guess I can take one for team Frost-DeLeon." She poked a finger into my chest. "Don't forget you owe me for this."

"I haven't. I'm looking forward to it," I said, throwing heat into my gaze. "I'm at your service. Use me any way you like."

"You're funny, DeLeon." Yet she wasn't laughing. She tilted her head toward the open door a few feet away from where we stood. "This is me. I've got computer lab."

I leaned into her and her eyes narrowed on me.

"Don't even think about it," she growled with enough feistiness that I smiled.

Sure I was messing with her, but she made it too much fun. I took hold of the strap of her backpack and drew her into me. Close, until we stood toe-to-toe. She smelled like peaches. Our eyes locked and held. "Just so you know, we might have to kiss at some point. To make this believable to all the doubters."

She took a step backward and flicked her gaze down to her gray high-top sneakers and over her cut off sweat pants. Her hand tugged at the bottom of her T-shirt advertising Bowl-o-Rama's annual bowl-a-thon for veterans. "Doubters. Of course."

"Whoa, Ali. That's not what I meant at all. I'm only talking about how sudden it was."

"Whatever. Either way, let's kick that can down the road," she said. "Way down."

"Fine with me. I was only preparing you. It goes without saying the kiss will only happen if you're okay with it. But sure, nothing we have to think about right now." Although after being around Ali for a few weeks now, part of me didn't want to kick it too far down the road. "I'll see you at lunch."

"Yeah, yeah, yeah. This couple thing sure is a lot of work." She rolled her eyes. "But let's start the lunch thing next week."

"Sure," I agreed with a nod.

"Awesome." She entered her science class without a backward glance.

Not going to lie, something deflated in my chest. I didn't realize until now that I'd been looking forward to spending more time with Ali. I spun around, hiked my backpack further up my right shoulder, and headed to my English class.

"Dax! What the heck, dude?" TJ called from behind me, so I paused long enough for him to catch up. "You are not going to believe the rumor going around about you."

"About me and Ali Frost?" I knew TJ would track me down

once he'd heard the news. The gossip had probably fried a few computers and cell phones getting spread around last night.

"Crazy, right?" He laughed.

"Like a fox. As far as you know, it's true." I grabbed his arm, pulling him along with me to class. Coach would have both our butts if we got marked tardy. "Between you and me—this is that other idea I mentioned to solve my Paige problem."

"So, it's not true?"

"Nope. But Ali's cool enough to help me out. So yep, me and Ali Frost, Jackson High School's hot new couple."

"I dig it," TJ said. "Let's hope it works. The faster the better."

"Exactly." Except, I was enjoying the back and forth with Ali. Enjoying getting to know her. Sure, I wanted this plan to work, but I wouldn't mind if it took a little while.

10

FOOTBALL COACHES SHOULDN'T PACK LUNCHES

Ali

"A" LUNCH, OCT 23, 11:31 A.M.

Lunchtime. Oh, how I hated the cafeteria. It was worse than the hallways. Much worse. If the hallways were like walking through a gauntlet, the cafeteria was like being locked up in jail. Not that I had been. Just a guess.

Twenty minutes of cool kids judging the heck out of everyone walking by while they laughed and acted like they owned the place. It was annoying to watch and not fun to be on the receiving end of their laughter.

What the cool kids didn't know was that most of us outcast nerds were happy to be excluded from their exclusive club. If being a snotty b-word were the "dues" you had to pay to join, it didn't seem worth it.

I stood near the entrance, scanning the football players' table for Dax. Eating with DeLeon would be fine. Some of the other football players were nice like Duke Schwiky in my calculus class. There were also a couple in my computer class who didn't act like total jerks. Most of the time. No, it was the fact that eating at Dax's table meant eating with the cheer-leaders too.

There probably were some nice girls on the cheerleading squad, but I didn't bother talking with any in my classes. That was on me. Armadillo, remember? Seeing Paige and her battalion armed with their weaponized put-downs and shun-ning tactics in action only confirmed that going solo was the safest path toward graduation.

Just then Dax and his friend TJ got to the table, lunch trays in their hands. Dax caught my eyes and jerked his head, motioning me over from across the room. I pulled in a deep breath and began weaving my way through the tables toward Dax.

"Ali! Over here!"

I stopped and spun my head toward the voice that had called me. Shani. She stood waving me over from a table next to the far wall.

"Come sit with us!" This time it was Gaby waving me over. The whole bowling team sat together.

I'd been eating outside by myself, but now that I was getting to know my teammates it would fun to sit with them. Only I couldn't today. I shook them off and tipped my head in Dax's direction. Like watching a tennis match, they glanced over and then back at me. Shani sent me a wink. Gaby held two thumbs up. Mari shot me an okay sign. Rowena frowned, her gaze moving over Dax's table before she nodded at me. Bhakti shrugged.

With my teammates' seal of approval, I squeezed my paper lunch bag tighter in my hand and wove the rest of the way to the table where Dax stood waiting for me.

"Ali." Dax gave me a look so hot he almost had me convinced he actually liked me. He was really pouring it on for Paige. Which worked for me since the faster Paige clued in, the faster Dax and I could "break up" and get back to our regularly scheduled program. After he helped me, of course. But I could pour on the sappy girlfriend too.

"Darling Dax." I blinked up at him with dewy-eyed adoration. I'd see his "baby" and raise him one.

He snickered but quickly turned it into one of those clearing your throat deals, but the look in his eyes said touché.

TJ slid over so Dax and I could squeeze onto the bench. Yes, we got the side-eye from most of the table. Except not from Paige and her posse. Definite glares from that direction.

"I almost didn't recognize you without your bowling ball," Gwen said.

"Jeepers, I'm so glad you did. That would have been such a loss," I said.

"Hi, Ali Frost," Kev said, giving me a huge smile.

"Hi, Kev." Kev was actually the only kid I'd made friends with at school. The guy was like sunshine in human form. I knew he had bad days like anyone else, but it was hard to keep Kev down long.

He cupped his hands together and held them out toward me. "Kev's ready."

I opened my lunch, digging around until I found the Twinkie and tossed it to him.

"Thanks," he said, tearing it open.

Dax's friends looked between me and Kev like they'd never seen high school kids share food before. Oh, wait. I knew what it was. They'd never noticed the daily transaction between me and Kev because they'd never noticed me. I elbowed Dax and flipped him a pointed look.

"Yes, I get it. Has anyone told you that you have sharp elbows?" He bumped his shoulder softly into mine. "Let's see what you have for lunch."

"The usual stuff. You know, sandwich, fruit, cookies." It's just that there was almost enough food to feed a two-hundred pound linebacker. Football coaches shouldn't pack lunches for their daughters. That's why I'd started giving Kev my Twinkies. I dumped my food out on the table and reached for my sandwich. Looked like a BLT today.

"OMG, is that a note on your banana?" Gwen grabbed up my banana faster than a rattlesnake strikes. And then she proceeded to read my banana-note out loud to everyone at the table. "'Tackle your day, kiddo! Dad.' Your dad writes you notes? That is freaking hilarious."

Yeah, I could tell by all the laughter up and down the table. Whatever.

"Aww, that's cute your daddy makes your lunches." Paige's voice held the smallest trace of haughty condescension. Not too noticeable, but enough not to miss. The Goldilocks amount of snottiness.

"What can I say? I'm a lucky girl." I meant it. I loved my dad. If taking care of me—making my lunch every day—gave him something solid to hang on to until he rebuilt his life… I was more than fine with that.

"I think it's cool," Dax said.

"Thanks. Now"—I held my hand out to Gwen—"hand over my banana-note and no one gets hurt."

Gwen tossed my banana over. "You're such a weirdo."

Dax wrapped his arm around my shoulders and pulled me in close. "I think the word you're looking for is unique. There's something sexy about a girl who's not afraid to be different."

Sexy? This awkward nerd? My heart sort of tripped at that. Of course, being pressed against the warmth and hardness of his body may have had something to do with it too. Get a grip. He's acting, dummy. I did my best to ignore the itchy feeling from the look of green-eyed resentment on Paige's face. The quicker she accepted that she and Dax were over, the sooner I could take the target off my back.

To that end, I needed to do "couple" things. Slight problem: I'd never been part of a couple. Yep, never had a boyfriend. I know, I know… You're shocked, right? You're looking at my cut off sweats and my "Grab Your Balls, Head to the Alley" T-shirt and wondering, how could that possibly be? So, I'd have to wing it.

"H—hey, Dax. Do you want to hit up the McDonald Observatory this weekend?" I ignored the snickers from around the table and pressed on. "I heard they have a new Coronado SolarMax 90 hydrogen-alpha telescope…"

One peek over at Paige, and sure enough she was glued to our conversation, a smug grin blossoming on her face. TJ leaned around Dax, his eyes wide at my lame attempt.

"The…um…the Orionid meteor shower is supposed to peak." I poked Dax's thigh under the table with my finger, warning him not to laugh.

"This weekend? We're both busy on Friday night," Dax said.

"You've got the football game. But why will I be busy?" I cocked an eyebrow at him.

"Because you'll be there to watch me play."

"I will? I mean, of course I will. Yeah, no. I meant Saturday."

"I'm busy Saturday too," he said.

Gwen and Paige both snickered.

"Then two Saturdays from now." Geez, did he want my help or not? "In or out, DeLeon?"

"Oh, I'm in. I'm all in."

Paige didn't look smug anymore. She blinked across at Dax looking sad and lost. I might not like her, but I felt a little sorry for her. Then I remembered the many times I'd heard her go full-throttle mean girl on some poor innocent kid. My sympathy dried right up.

"But why don't we drive to Davis Mountains Park instead?" Dax asked. "It's not an official dark sky sanctuary, but a class two. We can watch the shower from the bed of my truck."

"Or…we could do that." Me and Dax DeLeon under the

stars? That sounded weird even to my ears. No wonder everyone at the table gawked at us.

"Great. We have a date." Dax gave me a crooked smile.

Dax's smile was the smile that made girls around school giggle and blush. Yesterday I would have sworn an oath that I was immune to that smile. Immune to his charm.

The kaleidoscope of butterflies that took flight in my belly said that was a lie.

A big lie.

"I've got to go." I did need extra time to make it out to the portable classrooms behind the school for my next class. But what I really needed was to get away from Dax and his smile and the vision of us lying in his pick-up truck watching stars. Because in this vision we were holding hands. *Wrong, wrong, wrong.* I gathered up my leftovers and trash and stood.

Dax delayed me with his hand on mine.

"I'll see you after football practice. I mean, if you can make it."

"Are you kidding? That's like the best part of being the quarterback's girlfriend," I gushed. Then up and downed him with my gaze before adding, "Okay, maybe the second or third best part."

His lips wiggled like he wanted to laugh, but he held it together as I turned and left the cafeteria. I swung through the Language Arts hallway to grab my calculus book from my locker. I'd slammed it shut and was giving my lock one quick spin when someone called my name.

I twisted my head around to look and, oh wonderful, it was Paige. Sucking in a breath, I turned to face her head on, realizing I was holding my calculus book against my chest like a shield. The fire in Paige's eyes said a shield would come in handy right now.

She stopped three feet away, staring at me with narrowed eyes. "Dax is mine, Frosty. You are way out of your league.

Didn't you hear everyone laughing at you at the lunch table? You don't belong in our group. Get a clue. Dax is just trying to make me jealous."

"Dax and I have talked a lot about what we are to each other. He's not trying to make you jealous." Everything I said was true, and unlike Paige, I was trying to be nice. "Dax and I are together. Maybe it would hurt less if you accepted it and moved on."

"Accepted it?" Paige stepped into my space with a growl. "Oh my god, have you looked at yourself? You're a joke. Now stay away from Dax."

"Yeah, that's not going to happen," I said. Part of me was pissed that Paige thought she could treat people like this and get away with it. The other part of me wanted to roll back up into my solitary armor, safe and protected.

Maybe I needed to hurry up and have Dax meet my dad. Just in case. And let Dax handle his Paige problem by himself.

11

RULES FOR FOOTBALL GIRLFRIENDS

Dax

AFTER SCHOOL, 3:20 P.M.

I left my seventh period class and headed out to the parking lot to grab my football gear. I might've sped up the littlest bit with the chance that I could catch Ali before she left for bowling team practice.

Sure enough, she was halfway out to her car in the parking lot. It didn't take much jogging to catch up with her. Wrapping my arm around her waist, I pulled her in toward me, chest to chest. I'd surprised her and she looked up at me, the sunlight revealing flecks of gold in her eyes.

"Hey there. Just wanted to see you before both of us head off for practice."

"I guess this is a thing too, huh?" She shook her head at me.

"It is. But not too painful, right?" I brushed back a wild curl from her face.

She sucked in a breath of air. "No. I think I'll live. Is there a minimum time that we have to stand here like this?"

I laughed. This girl was killing me. "Yes. 10 seconds should do it. We're still early days yet. Give us another week or two and it might take more time than that."

"Do you really think this is going to take a couple weeks?" She squinted up at me trying to keep the sun out.

I nodded. "Yeah, I do. I broke up with Paige five months ago, and she's still acting like we're just on a break. No matter how many times I've tried to set her straight. So, yeah."

"Okay. As long as I know what I'm in for," she said. "Ten seconds. My work here is done."

"Who's counting?" I grinned and shook my head at her. "You missed my football game last week."

"Then we're even because you missed my bowling competition." Ali raised an eyebrow at me. "And now it's definitely been over ten seconds, so have a great practice."

"Hang on now." I pulled her closer. "You haven't had a bowling meet yet this season."

"True." She shrugged. "But you pulled the guilt card, so I figured it was worth a shot."

"You called me out. Fair enough." I stood back as we separated, running my hand down along her arm until only our hands touched. I interlocked my fingers with hers. "Did you mean it when you said you'd come by at the end of practice? Or was that just for show?"

"OMG, yes!" She released an exaggerated sigh and blinked her eyes up at me. "I'm super excited. I wouldn't miss it for anything."

I laughed and squeezed her hand lightly. "You are hard on a guy's ego."

"Pretty sure your ego can take it." She pulled her hand away, turned her back on me and continued on toward her car, leaving me standing there like a lovesick fool. Which was fine because that's what I was supposed to look like. She threw her hand up in a casual wave without turning around. "Later for me."

I grabbed my equipment from my truck, got dressed, and hustled out on the field. Coach made the last five players to arrive on the field for practice cleanup at the end. Snack wrappers, water bottles, dropped towels. It wasn't a terrible job but after a long hard practice in the heat of the Texas afternoon it wasn't a fun job either. I was never one of the last five on the field. TJ found me on the sidelines warming up with some stretches.

"How's your girlfriend doing?" TJ tossed his bag down next to mine before joining me doing stretches.

"Awesome." I grinned. "Paige hasn't taken the hint yet, but it hasn't been a hardship getting to know Ali."

"Did you know your girlfriend is the top bowler on the varsity team?"

"No. Not a surprise though since I've seen her bowl. How did you find out?"

"You're kidding, right? When Dax DeLeon starts dating some chick no one's even heard of, people are going to talk. She's not only the top bowler at our school... She made All-State last year."

"Holy cow. To think I didn't even know we had a bowling team." I knew she was wicked-good from bowling class. Not that she showed off. She didn't. She quietly and steadily prac-ticed during class. She never criticized anyone else's form. Huh. "My girlfriend's a hotshot athlete."

"Whoa. Athlete? Dude, she's a bowler."

"Obviously you've never seen her bowl."

Coach blew his whistle and we started practice. After stretching and warm-ups we split up into individual positions for focused practice. We worked on a new play—one of Coach D's trick plays—which we hoped would add an element of surprise when we were down and needed a score.

"Dax, try that again. Way to hit your mark, TJ. Let's try the other side," Coach said. "As quarterback, you've got to assess it quicker, Dax. When that play starts falling apart, don't hesitate to call an audible. You're the captain of the ship."

"Got it." Don't hesitate. Captain the ship.

Grady walked up to me and grabbed my facemask. "You'll get it. Just stop thinking so much."

That's exactly what I did. For the rest of practice, I stopped overthinking every play. I got out of my own way and sure enough I did better. I hit my receivers and scrambled plays on the fly. I needed to stop thinking about scouts in the stands and let go of the guilt from last year. Heck, we'd made it to the championship game for the first time in our school's history. It wasn't even like my teammates were pissed anymore.

By the time Coach blew the whistle ending practice, I felt better. Steadier.

"Good job, Dax." Coach tapped his fist on my shoulder pads. "Play like that in the games and we'll be the team to beat heading into playoffs."

"That's the plan, Coach."

"Between DeLeon as our QB, Coach D's secret plays, and Cox still hurting for coaches, there is no doubt we'll win the championship this year," Parker, our ever-cocky strong safety crowed.

"Don't count your football trophies until you've earned them," Coach said.

Parker was cocky, but he was right about Cox. The only reason we'd beat them in the playoffs last year was due to some big coaching shakeup. It had thrown them off their game and helped us win. The word was they still hadn't solved their coaching problem.

After downing two cups of water, I gathered my gear and my bag. I turned my gaze to the bleachers, looking for Ali. She was easy to find, her red hair lit up like living flames in the sunshine.

I sent her a nod and she responded by blowing me a big kiss. Yep, that was my girl.

I walked over to meet her but before I even got halfway Paige and Gwen sat down next to her. That couldn't be good. Whatever Paige said wiped the smile off Ali's face.

I needed to put an end to that quickly. "Hey, Ali! Get your cute, little behind down here!"

Both Ali and Paige turned to look at me. Ali pointed a finger against her chest.

"You can't be talking to me," she said. By this time, I'd reached the bottom of the bleachers.

"Would you please, Ali Frost"—I held my hand out toward her—"come down here."

"Oh, absolutely." She side-eyed Paige. "Your timing couldn't be more perfect."

Well, that was the whole point of the "cute, little behind" comment. To get her attention quickly so I could help her escape.

Ali moved down the bleachers so fast she looked like she was doing a stair workout. I reached out my hand, helping her down the last step.

"Well, that was fun," Ali said. "Not."

"I'm sorry. I did rescue you though."

"My hero." She looked up at me, fluttering her eyelashes. "But seriously, was that it? Girlfriends stop by to drool over your muscles?"

"Number one: you don't just drool over my muscles. You're also impressed with my football skills. And maybe my muscles. Number two: that's not it. I mean, when it's real—when a guy and girl are serious—then sometimes there's a kiss at the end of practice."

"Oh. I guess if I were serious about a guy—about you—it might be worth sitting through the end of practice for a kiss."

"Might be?" I gave a light tug to her ponytail. "If we were

serious about each other my kiss would totally be worth it. You can take that to the bank."

"Wow, DeLeon. We're going to need to work on your confidence."

"My confidence?"

"Oh yeah. Gonna need to deflate it before you float away."

12

GOLDFISH OR BARRACUDAS?

Ali

WEDNESDAY @ BOWLING PRACTICE, OCT 30

The girls hit me with questions as soon as I got to practice.

"How is lunch with Dax going?" Bhakti asked.

"Fine."

"We need more than 'fine.' Did he give you a bite of his food? That's a sign he's moving things to the next step." Mari nodded. "I read it in a magazine at my dentist's office."

"No. No bite of food was shared." I mean, yikes. "I certainly didn't share a bite of my food."

"That's good. You should play hard to get. Make him go first," Rowena said. "That's what I'd do so I wouldn't have to be afraid of him rejecting me."

"Thanks. I'll remember that."

"What about Paige? Is she managing to be nice?"

"Nice?" *Dax is mine, Frosty. You're a joke. Stay away from Dax.* "Paige is…Paige."

"So, no. Figures."

Coach blew her whistle, waving us down to lane fifteen and we started practice.

We were halfway through bowling practice, about to begin ISD, when Mari elbowed me in my side.

"Um... Ali."

"What? Is it my turn?" I didn't think it was but I'd been mentally going through my form for picking up a spare and I might have lost track.

"No. I think it's safe to say, thanks to you, everyone in school finally knows Jackson High School has a bowling team." She flashed me a big smile and tilted her head behind me.

I turned around and was absolutely surprised to find Dax standing at the edge watching me. He was dressed for practice in athletic shorts and a Jackson football T-shirt. He shrugged and leaned one shoulder against a pillar as if settling in for a long while.

I left my lane and moved over to where he stood by the bowling ball racks. "What are you doing here?"

"Short practice because of our game tomorrow night. I thought over what you said. Why shouldn't the guy go watch his girl do her thing?"

"Thank you, I guess. But you do realize Paige isn't here to see this, right?"

"Are you kidding? It's probably been texted 20 times in the last five minutes that my truck is at Bowl-O-Rama. She knows." He gave a light tug on the hem of my T-shirt. "Besides, when I said I enjoy watching you bowl, it was no lie. You're good."

"Thanks." My stomach twisted like a hard spin of a bowling ball and I wasn't sure if it was from his compliment or the tug on my T-shirt. Possibly both.

"How did you get into bowling?" he asked. "Do your parents bowl?"

"No. It was my nana. She was in a bowling league. When I was little, she watched me when my parents were at work." The memories of the time spent with my nana were sweet. "I was an honorary member of the Knitting Grannies bowling team before I turned twelve."

Dax laughed. "I bet you were adorable."

"More like adorkable. But I wouldn't change that time of my life for anything." I shrugged. "Plus, I'm hoping for a bowling scholarship to help pay for college."

"I didn't know they had those."

"Not many, but enough to give me hope."

"You coming to the game on Friday?" He ran a finger along the protective tape I had on my thumb. "It's an away game."

"I don't know." I shrugged. I actually loved football. I'd grown up around it. But I hadn't been to a game since my mom's affair went public.

"I'd like you to." His dark brown, almost black gaze cajoled. "How about this? How about I buy you a ticket and leave it at the ticket office?"

"No. Don't—"

"No pressure. If you can make it, great." He wrapped his large hand around mine, rubbing his thumb lightly over my palm. I didn't know my palm regulated my lungs until that moment when I suddenly was short of breath. "I'd like you to wear my jersey."

"Um…" I blinked up at him, so busy trying to breathe that I was having trouble thinking straight. "Won't you be wearing it?"

He grinned and tugged my shirt hem again. "I have more than one. Hey, it's a thing girlfriends do—wear their boyfriend's jersey."

"Oh, right. Like I'm just another adoring fan." That didn't sound remotely like something I wanted to do. "I'm going to pass on that. It sounds too much like fan-girling for my personal football star."

"Fan-girling? No. To me, when a girl wears her guy's jersey, it's personal. It represents the unique special connection no other girl has to the guy. I don't know. Like the guy is shouting out to the world, 'That's my girl. That's the one who has my heart.' And the girl is saying, 'That's my guy and I want everyone to know it.'"

"Yikes. Sounds a little possessive." Granted, I'd never been in a serious relationship, but the whole "shout out to the world" thing sounded dramatically excessive. "I mean, why don't I just get your name tattooed on my body? Or heck, I could go old-school and brand your initials on my—"

"Okay, okay. I get it." He laughed and pulled me into his chest and hugged me. "It's a definite no on wearing my jersey. I'd settle for you coming to the game."

"Frost!"—I jerked out of Dax's arms—"That's another demerit! Get your flirt on during your own time." Coach frowned at us both. "DeLeon? What are you doing here?"

"Hi, Coach Diamond. I stopped by to watch my girl bowl."

"Well you're a distraction. Take a hike."

"Sorry about that." Dax pointed at me. "I'll talk to you later."

"Oh, and DeLeon... A win would be nice this Friday."

"Yes, ma'am. That's the plan."

Dax left, but not before throwing me a wink and his lopsided smile. The whole team watched him leave.

"Oooh, giiirrrl. That boy is fine." Shani bumped her shoulder into mine.

"Holy cow, Ali," Gaby said.

Yep. Holy cow was right. Even though it was all an act, my heart rate spiked a little. Okay, a lot.

"Frost, you've got BPD after practice. Now, how about we get back to work? I for one want to beat the cowboy boots off of Navarro next week."

Coach worked her way down the line giving us each our highlight items and weak areas to work on. We settled down, refocused, and worked hard because we wanted to beat Navarro too.

We skipped the normal fifteen minutes of fun time. Coach said to blame me for disrupting our practice, but the girls only giggled and gave me a thumb's up when Coach wasn't looking.

"All right, ladies, bring it in!" Coach called. "Let's talk about what happened last season. Frost had a great season, but we lost the team competition. And I want it, girls. I want it bad. I know you can do this. Stop bowling safe. Get fierce. Stop being nice. Get ferocious. Dig deep. Find something that makes you mad—no, not just mad. Find something that pisses you off—and channel that anger into your bowling. Roll hard. If you can't do it for yourself—do it for me. I need you to be barracudas, not goldfish!

"I want to plant our bowling trophy front and center in the trophy case." Coach ripped Mari's wiping cloth out of her hands and stood on a chair. Putting one foot up on the chair back, she waved the towel over her head. "Like a flag on Mt. Everest. I want every student and teacher who passes through Jackson High School to know we ascended to the highest peak in the bowling world."

Huh. I was afraid that would be an unscaled mountain. Not that we weren't trying to win the team competitions. We were. Somehow though when the competition got close, we sort of morphed into a bunch of nice girls who bowled. Goldfish.

"That's it for today. Frost?" Coach handed me the polishing kit with an evil grin. "Have fun and make them shine."

After all the girls apologized for not being able to stay late and help, which I wouldn't have let them if they could since it was my fault, I got to work. I replayed Dax's wink through my mind and ball polishing duties didn't seem like that bad of a trade-off.

Which was not a good thing. I had a stern conversation with myself. You're an idiot, Ali Frost, if you forget this isn't real. That wink. That smile. They're not really yours, so forget them.

Dax didn't like me and I didn't like him. I mean, I liked him.

It turned out he was pretty nice. But I didn't like him-like him. Noooo. Uh-uh.

Dax had a plan and I had a plan. We'd joined forces. That was all this was.

I shoved all things Dax out of my head and focused on polishing. I ran my bowling form through my head like a movie so I could look for flaws.

Flaws and places to tweak my game to take it to a higher level. Because I couldn't forget the other half of my plan. Of course, first was to make sure my dad was okay. Once my dad was living his life again, I planned to escape this small town where everyone knew our sad story. Where even a year later people still whispered behind our backs. Where people still threw me angry looks over the football championship they didn't have. The only way I could afford to go away to college was to get a bowling scholarship.

Almost two hours later, when the high school bowlers had given way to the adult bowling leagues, I finally finished BPD. Okay, fine, BPD didn't take me that long, but I ended up sharing a plate of loaded nachos from the snack bar with the Knitting Grannies while they grilled me about school. After getting hugs from the whole team I left the alley. The sun was already below the tree line leaving a shadowy twilight to settle in.

At my car I opened my trunk and looked at the mess. It used to be organized. Over the last year — just like my life — it had turned into a jumbled mess. It gave "junk in your trunk" new meaning.

I let out a puff of air, set my bowling ball bag and shoes on the ground, and got to work. Making space in this mess was definitely a two-handed job. I refused to cave and store stuff on my backseat. Cramming everything in my trunk meant I'd have to deal with the mess someday. Someday soon, from the looks of it. I slid my library books toward the back and shoved the stack of T-shirts I'd scored at 2nd Time Around, my favorite vintage store to the—

Whoa! Someone grabbed me from behind, pushing my shoulders down until the side of my face pressed against the pile of shirts in my trunk. My heart pounded and my breath hitched. *Was I being robbed?* Devil's Lap was a small town with small-time crime. The worst we had were kids street racing or a fight at the local bar.

This couldn't be happening. But another shove on my shoulders made it clear... It was happening! Think, Ali, think.

"Where's the playbook?"

13

TWO GOONS WALK INTO A PARKING LOT

Ali

"Where's the playbook?" A guy's voice growled in my ear. "Don't make me ask you again!"

"I have no idea what you're talking about!" I twisted my head as far as I could while being held down. In the murky darkness all I could glimpse were two dudes. The one holding me down and another slurping on a Scoops milkshake while he peered into my bowling ball bag. They wore baseball caps pulled low, making it impossible to see their faces. "Stop messing with my bag! Bowlers don't have playbooks!"

"Oh, you're gonna play dumb now? Not bowling. Football." The guy gave my shoulders a shake. Not hard, but just enough to let me know he was serious. "We had a deal. Now... Where's the playbook?"

"A football playbook? How would I know?" I didn't have enough space to kick backward with sufficient force to hurt the guy. The worst I could do was maybe a stomp on his foot. One glance down made that plan moot. My size six to his size gargantuan? Yeah, no. "You've got the wrong girl."

"You the coach's daughter?"

"What?"

"Just answer the question." Another shake on my shoulders. "Is your dad a coach?"

"Yes, but—"

"Are you the quarterback's girlfriend?"

"No. I mean, yes. Sort of. It's complicated."

Goon #2 pulled the lid off his shake and tipped it, slowly pouring it into my bowling bag.

"Don't do that!" I stomped on Goon #1's foot anyway. No reaction. "Come on, dude. Stop. That's my lucky Ninja ball. It was my nana's."

"Stop playing dumb. You're going to get us the playbook, or else…"

"Or else what?" The jerks. I doubted I'd get all the milkshake out of my ball. Not easily anyway. "You've already ruined my lucky bowling ball."

The guy moved the cup over and poured the rest of the shake into my bowling shoes.

"They don't make those shoes anymore. They matched our school colors perfectly."

"You think this is a joke?" Goon #2 growled. I figured it was a rhetorical question and he didn't want a response. "You're going to find out real soon how serious we are."

"Get the playbook," Goon #1 threatened and then he stomped on my foot which hurt, darn it.

The goons took off on a run while I leaned my forehead against the T-shirts waiting for the intense pain to subside. Their footsteps signaled their exit to the parking lot behind Bowl-O-Rama and off toward the abandoned gas station.

I stood and took a tentative step on my aching foot. I probably had a bruise the size of Texas but nothing felt broken. Hobbling over to my shoes and ball bag, I dumped out as much of the milkshake as I could before cramming them into my trunk and slamming it closed.

Idiots. Jerks. Those two Neanderthals were why the "football players are dumb jocks" stereotype existed. By the time I pulled in my driveway, my foot had stopped throbbing. Talk about being in the wrong place at the wrong time. The goons were too dumb to understand they had the wrong girl.

Pulling my bowling stuff from my trunk along with my backpack, I went inside, heading straight past the kitchen and down the hall to my room.

"Hey, kiddo! Dinner in ten minutes!" my dad called on my way by.

"Okay." If I washed my ball and shoes quickly, I might be able to salvage them. I had two other pairs of bowling shoes and two other balls but that didn't make me any less angry about what those goons had done.

Setting the ball and shoes in the tub, I got to work cleaning out what I could.

If I'd seen their faces or one of their vehicles, I'd report them. But it wouldn't do any good with only my word on it. Not after the breakdown I'd had last year. I think my dad knew it was an emotional breakdown because his heart had taken a beating too. The school psychologist had a different opinion, though, and her report had suggested a mental breakdown. Not hardly.

I pulled a slow breath in through my nose, finding my inner calm and pushing the whole weird encounter out of my mind. A lot of things were finally going right in my life. I wasn't going to let a couple of dumb jerks and a case of mistaken identity mess with that. They were someone else's problem. Not mine. My shoes were probably unrecoverable, but I could get my bowling ball professionally cleaned.

I set everything upside-down on a towel to drain and joined my dad for dinner.

"Perfect timing," he said, sliding two plates onto the table. We ate most meals at the kitchen island, but Dad insisted one meal each week had to be at the table. Maybe it was his need to make our lives feel more normal. "Grab the ketchup and mustard from the fridge, will you?"

"Sure." I grabbed them both along with a jar of pickles. Cheeseburgers were one of the handful of dishes my dad did well. "Oh, yum. I love cheeseburger night."

"How was school today?" he asked. They were the same questions he used to ask before mom left, yet different. Because he wasn't asking about school but about me. He needed to see I was fine. That what mom had put us through hadn't done permanent damage.

"Good. Great even." I ate a few bites before adding, "I'm going to the football game Friday night."

"You are? That's great." My dad's mouth curled into a small, satisfied smile. "It's good to see you get involved in your new school."

I ate some steamed broccoli while enjoying the happy look on Dad's face.

"How's bowling going? You've got your first competition next week."

"Yeah, Navarro. Coach is hyped up already. I volunteered to have the team pizza party at our house. Saturday afternoon." That sat my dad back in his chair. "Is that okay?"

Dad laughed. "It's absolutely okay. So, Saturday. Yeah, that works."

"Yep. We won't get crazy and make a huge mess. I mean, how crazy can six bowling nerds get?"

* * *

November 1, Friday 8:10 a.m.

Friday morning, I sat in computer lab, tired and cranky. Why was I tired and cranky? Because instead of a good night's sleep I'd tossed and turned with dreams of Dax. Dax taking my hand and leaning into me. Dax making my heart flutter like a flag in the wind. A delicious dream until Paige popped up and chased after me. I woke up as a twenty-foot tall Paige knocked me away with a giant bowling ball.

That had to be why I was cranky. It couldn't be because it was "B" day which meant I wouldn't see Dax in bowling class. Nope. That kind of thinking was ridiculous. Dax didn't mean anything to me.

Dax and I aren't real. Dax and I aren't real. Dax and I aren't real. I forced myself to remember that while the morning announcements droned on over the PA system.

Juniors: the deadline to sign up for the SAT is next week.

Was my life better than it had been a year ago? Even six months ago? Yes. Better. Some things were beginning to settle into a comfortable rhythm.

The marching band is having a fundraiser by selling candy bars at lunch today. Let's everyone help them get to the BOA competition.

Somehow, I'd moved from simply trying to survive another day to actually looking forward to the day ahead at school. Was that because of my growing friendship with my teammates? Or because of Dax DeLeon?

Don't forget the pep rally at 3 o'clock this afternoon. Our own Jackson Jackalopes face off against the Navarro Night Owls at seven thirty tonight. Come on out and cheer them on.

Pep rally? Yeah, no. I told Dax I'd go to the football game, but I wasn't doing the pep rally.

That's all for the announcements today. Have a great day and —

This is Principal Barstow with an urgent announcement. Our beloved school mascots, Mr. and Ms. Jackalope, are missing. If this is a senior prank, return them by lunchtime and no one will get in trouble. That is all.

The mascots were missing? Whoa. Kids had done some crazy stuff for senior pranks, but even from the short time I'd been at Jackson High I knew the mascots were special. Almost sacred even. Something about their lineage going all the way back to the first day of Jackson High. Some kid was either very brave or very stupid.

"Oh my." Ms. Baxter's hand fluttered in the air. "Has anyone heard a rumor about this? Mr. and Ms. Jackalope are a delicate breed of rabbit. Anyone?"

I looked around waiting to see if anyone was going to respond. Nothing.

"All right. Let's move on. Please open your books to page two-hundred and eleven…"

After forty-five minutes of talking about Excel spreadsheets and handling a pop quiz, Ms. Baxter let us go. The hallways had that extra-excited Friday buzz going on. Threading my way through the crowded hallway I caught snatches of conversations. *OMG, do you know who stole the mascots? Catch a ride to tonight's football game? Head's up, pop quiz in Baxter's class. Huge party this Saturday! Gonna be epic, man.*

Like a salmon trying to swim against the stream, I pushed out of the flow of traffic to my locker to exchange textbooks. Even with the haphazard mess of my locker, I saw it right away. The folded-up note that had been slipped through the slats.

Seeing a folded note resting on top of my books was all it took to throw me back into the past. Back to daily notes full of vicious taunts and crude, vile suggestions of things I should do or places I should go. My stomach tumbled and sloshed like an overflowing washing machine. My pulse stuttered. Oh, god. Please not again.

Except…that didn't make sense. No one here cared about my old high school losing. Cox was one of Jackson High's biggest rivals. The kids at Jackson were more likely to throw me a ticker tape parade for being the reason Cox had collapsed last year. No. It wasn't the start of those malicious notes again.

Calm down. Breathe.

With a deep breath, I relaxed and let go of the tension, letting it slide away like a wave on the beach disappeared into the ocean. A simple note from a friend. It had been so long since I'd had friends, I'd all but forgotten that's what friends did. Now that my teammates were friends, I could enjoy that again. I bet it was Shani or Gaby. I even knew how Shani's note would begin... *Giiirrrl.* I grinned and opened the note.

Guess what? It wasn't from one of my friends. Not even close. The note was a collection of letters cut from newspapers and magazines into words.

Bring the Playbook. Or Else. Old Devil's Bridge. Saturday 12:00 Midnight. Come Alone.

Under that was a picture of Mr. and Ms. Jackalope.

What the freaking heck? This could not be serious. It had to be a joke. A stupid, cruel joke. Whoa, wait. The two goons from the bowling alley. Probably not a joke. Those two idiots *still* didn't get that they had the wrong girl. I folded the note and shoved it into my backpack to throw away at home. I wasn't taking a chance of someone seeing me toss it into the trash at school.

I felt bad for the rabbits, but this wasn't my problem. Nope.

The girl who'd made the rat-faced, weaselly deal to give the jerks the playbook would have to deal with it, but not me.

My relief was short-lived though because I couldn't ignore the fear that clawed at me. If something happened to those rabbits, I might be blamed.

I'd already been the most hated girl at one school.

Was I about to become the most hated girl at Jackson High School too?

14

GET OUT OF YOUR HEAD!

Dax

FRIDAY NIGHT FOOTBALL GAME, NOV 1, 8:45 P.M.

Fourth quarter of the game and we were up twenty-one to
seventeen. I'd played a solid first half. The second half wasn't
going as great. Some reporter from the local paper had called to
me on our way to the locker room at half-time. He wanted to
know how I handled the pressure of knowing a Texas Tech
recruiter was watching.

How did I handle it? By not knowing. That was how.

Now that I knew, I couldn't get it out of my head. I mean, no
pressure. Just the recruiter from my dad's alma mater. Just the
chance to mess up the dream my dad had been talking about
forever. The dream we'd both held on to for years. Knowing he
was in the stands was all it took to have me second guessing
every move I made.

Get out of your head. Focus.

We caught a lucky break when Navarro fumbled the ball and
Vasquez recovered it for us on the forty-yard line. All I had to
do was move it down field for a touchdown.

I stood behind Jake, our center, with my knees bent and hands out. I looked right and left, scoping out where their guys were lined up. "Blue, 32! Blue, 32! Hut!"

Jake snapped the ball to me and I took my two steps back while I checked on my receivers. TJ had a guy all over him, but Grady slipped past his guy and into an open lane. A flash of movement to my left surged toward me. Rushing to avoid being sacked, I unloaded the ball, throwing a sweet spiral to Grady.

Only Grady wasn't the one who caught it. Nope. A Navarro player came out of nowhere, snagging my pass out of the air, surprising everyone.

Dammit. I pulled myself together enough to take after the guy as he ran past the forty...the thirty...the twenty...the ten. I finally brought him down on the seven-yard line.

As I jogged off the field, I ran the play through my head trying to figure out where I'd made my mistake. Was my timing off? Did I overthrow it? Did it get tipped?

Thanks to our strong defense, the other team failed to score from my mistake. We scored a rushing touchdown and won the game. I was happy for our team, but not happy at all with my own performance.

"We won! High five!" Kev grinned at me and raised his hand, as always, our number one cheerleader.

"We did." I shoved my personal disappointment down and slapped my hand to his. "Thanks to our defense we came out on top."

Thirty minutes later, I left the locker room intent on finding Ali. She said she'd be at the game and wait for me after. Just the thought of her had me grinning.

"Great game, Dax!"

"Hey, thanks," I said, walking through the gauntlet of pats on my shoulder and "good jobs" all the while scanning my gaze through the crowd. I found Ali leaning against the wall next to the equipment room.

I changed my angle, purposefully cutting through the crowd of students, parents, and alumni. My eyes steady on hers. When I was within five feet, she pushed herself away from the wall to meet me halfway when Paige bounced between us, looking perkier than her cheerleading pompoms.

"Baby, you were awesome out there!" She threw herself against me, wrapping her arms around my neck like an octopus around prey.

"Thanks." Without breaking eye contact with Ali, I unwound Paige's arms, set her to the side, and closed the gap between us. She wasn't dressed up with blown dried hair and tight jeans like a lot of the girls. Her hair was up in a messy bun although a few wild, red curls had slid free. She was swallowed up in an over-sized Army jacket big enough to fit her father. It struck me that what I liked about Ali was how completely genuine she was. "You made it."

"I did."

Some teammates joined us. TJ, Grady, and a couple others along with some of the cheerleaders. Post-game dissections and directions to "the" Friday night party buzzed around, fading into background noise. I was focused on Ali.

"What did you think of the game?" I asked her.

"Oh, um, good." She flashed me an over-bright smile. "You won, so yay."

"Seriously, Frosty? That's all you've got? Dax was amazing tonight, but I guess you bowling nerds don't know enough about football to get that."

Paige hovered around us like an annoying mosquito looking for a place to bite so she could suck the life force out of her next victim.

I took Ali's hand in mine and winked at her. Our private joke that did exactly what I'd hoped—made her relax and smile.

"Everyone's heading to the party at Josh's." Paige glanced at my hand—the one holding Ali's—and her face hardened before lifting her gaze up to me. "Want us to wait for you?"

"No. My bowling nerd and I have other plans." I wrapped my arm around Ali's shoulders, tucked her up next to me, and guided us away with a wave to the guys.

Our other plans were milkshakes and burgers sitting on my open tailgate at the edge of an apple orchard a few miles outside of town. It was cool out, but not cold. We weren't "parked" as in making-out parked. It was simply that it was one of my favorite spots.

"Are these apple trees?" Ali asked, peering down a line of trees. "I didn't know apples grew around here."

"Best apples in Texas. Wait 'til you taste one." I opened our take-out bag, took out our three burgers—one for Ali, two for me—and dumped the fries into the bag, setting it between us. "Of course, you'll have to wait until next season."

Her gaze moved around taking in the row upon row of trees. "How did you ever find this place?"

"This is my Tía Angelina's orchard." I glanced around, listening to the quiet rustle of leaves. "When I was in elementary school I used to climb in this orchard like a monkey."

"It's nice." She looked around, swinging her feet, only to freeze and turn toward me. "Unless this is where you bring all your girlfriends. Then it's a bit creepy."

"Nope. You're the first girl I've brought here." Which was weird now that I thought about it. "I come here to escape. To think."

"Gotcha. I go to the bowling alley to escape or figure things out."

We started on our food, enjoying the cool, quiet night. The moon was bright, hiding some stars but lighting up Ali's face.

"What is it tonight?" Ali sipped her milkshake. "Escaping? Or thinking?"

"A bit of both, I guess." I'd been having issues for almost a year now on the football field and hadn't told a soul. Something about Ali made it easy to open up. "It's just—sure we won tonight, but I almost blew the game for us."

"You made a mistake. You're human. I bet everyone on the field tonight made a mistake."

"Maybe, but a quarterback's mistakes can lose the game. Like tonight's interception. Or last week's fumble." I shook my head, biting into my second burger while I gathered my thoughts. "I'm pissed at myself. That interception was avoidable. I know it. My team knows it. Sure as heck the recruiter in the stands knows it."

"A recruiter in the stands? What school?"

"Only my dream school, Texas Tech. My dad's alma mater."

"Okay. That's a lot of pressure."

"Pressure. Yeah. I let it get into my head and it throws me off my game." I crumpled the empty wrapper in my hand, wadding it up in a tight fist. "I've dreamed of following in my dad's footsteps since I played Pop Warner."

"So, take some pressure off."

"I'm all ears." Maybe Ali was the wrong person to talk to. I mean, what kind of pressure had she dealt with? Bowling was worlds away from football. At least in Texas. In Texas, football was everything. "The pressure to win, impress recruiters, and get a football scholarship are real. I can't make them disappear."

"I sort of think you can. What's your backup plan?" she asked.

"What are you talking about?"

"Your backup plan if a football scholarship doesn't work out."

"I've got one plan. Football. Football has been my life since before middle school. It's all I've dreamed about. It's all my family has dreamed about. You don't think I'm good enough?"

"I didn't say that. All I'm saying is it might be a good idea to have a fallback in case the football thing doesn't work."

"That's like planning to fail. That's not how I roll. I focus like a laser on a goal and throw everything I have toward it." I jumped off the tailgate, grabbed an apple from the ground, and threw it into the darkness. "Then when I've done my best and the cards are dealt, I'll see what I've got."

"I respect the passion, but if the pressure is affecting your game, then your method isn't working, is it?"

"What about you? What if you don't get a bowling scholarship?" I asked, shoving my hands into the back pockets of my jeans. Maybe I was a little defensive. "What's your backup plan?"

"I've got three. Community college, work full-time until I have enough to pay for college, or go to trade school, like welding or something."

"You want to be a welder?" I tipped my head down and gave her one of those "get real" looks.

"No, I don't want to be a welder." She rolled her eyes at me. "But it's a viable option that pays enough to live on. Bowling scholarships are rare and competitive. I have better odds of winning the lottery than a scholarship. Bowling isn't like football where they practically toss money at you like confetti in a parade."

"If you won the lottery"—I moved in close, resting my hands on the tailgate on either side of her hips, and leaned in—"you wouldn't need a scholarship."

"Very funny." Ali laughed and pushed my chest to get me out of her face. "Fine. Win the lottery. Now I've got four backup plans. What do you have?"

What did I have? Outside of football—not much.

"Apparently, a lot of thinking to do."

15

BOWLERS HAVE BALLS

Ali

PIZZA PARTY, NOV 2, 1 P.M.

"Are ten pizzas enough?"

"You did not order ten pizzas. Dad! I said seven girls, not a football team."

"I wanted to make sure your friends get enough to eat. Plus, I had to cover everyone. Meat lovers, vegetarian, gluten-free, kosher, nondairy."

"Dad, I love you. Especially this new mushy side of you I've never seen."

"I have no idea what you're talking about. I'm a mean, crusty old football coach. I don't do mushy."

"Of course you don't. But seriously, it's just a few friends." I sent him a warning look. "Don't get weird."

"Define weird."

I crossed my arms over my chest and sent him my "oh no you don't" look.

"Kidding. I'm kidding. I'll be as cool as I can manage. But

between you and me, this is a good thing, kiddo. You're making friends again. It's good."

The doorbell rang, sending Bella sprinting to the front door with a bark. Dad got a funny look on his face. It was the same look he had when I played a flowerpot in the school play in kindergarten.

"Dad..."

"I'm cool. Totally cool. Not being weird. Is it okay if I light the fire pit for you and your friends? It's a nice place to hang out."

"That would be okay. Thanks." Dad headed out back while I took hold of Bella's collar and opened the front door to welcome the first teammate who'd arrived. But it wasn't just one of them. It was the whole team. "Did you all carpool together?"

"Yeah. We always do," Shani said. "Gaby doesn't have her license since she's an exchange student. Ro is afraid to drive. Mari says carpooling today means our kids will have a planet tomorrow and Bhakti has to share her mom's van with her sister."

"So, it's usually Shani." Gaby shrugged. "But now that you're going to be hanging out with us, we can squeeze into your Volvo. Which is retro cute, by the way."

"Thanks. Come on in. Is everyone okay with a dog?" Bella sat whining, her tail swishing at full speed on the floor.

"We're fine." Gaby held her hand out. "Come here, pretty girl."

Bella happily soaked up the attention.

"She's adorable," Shani said.

"She's also a thief, so watch your shoes and zip up your purses." I led the way to the back of the house. "I hope you guys are hungry because my dad went overboard on ordering pizza."

"I ran three miles around the track, so I'm hungry," Mari said. "Oh, but I don't eat dairy, meat, or eggs."

"Got you a vegan pizza," I said. "Let's grab some drinks from the fridge and carry the pizzas out back."

We raided the refrigerator on our way through the kitchen, grabbing drinks and a bowl full of grapes. After lifting the lids on the pizza boxes everyone found a pizza they liked and carried them outside. It looked like Dad had finished getting the fire pit going.

"Dad, I want you to meet my friends. Shani, Gaby, Mari, Rowena, and Bhakti, meet my dad."

"Girls." My dad gave them a nod and a smile. "Great to meet you."

"You too, Mr. Frost," Mari said. "Oh, I love the fire pit."

My dad stood like his feet had rooted to the ground until I cleared my throat and jerked my head toward the house.

"Right. I've got stuff, important stuff, to do inside. You girls enjoy." He gave me a wink on his way into the house.

It was quiet for a second until the door shut behind Dad, and then they all turned to me wide-eyed.

"That's your dad?" Shani asked. "I've seen him at our competitions, but I didn't know he was your dad!"

"Holy moly! I hope this doesn't sound weird, but your dad is hot," Gaby said. "Smoking hot."

"He looks like Chris Pine, only older." Bhakti blinked, still staring at the door like she was waiting for another peek.

Rowena sighed. "Your mom is a lucky woman."

My shoulders stiffened and I sucked in a breath. "My parents are divorced. It's just me and my dad."

"He doesn't have a girlfriend?" Shani asked. "That's crazy."

"The divorce wasn't that long ago. And it was kind of sudden." I put two pieces of pepperoni pizza on my plate and moved over to one of the chairs that circled the fire pit. "I don't think he's ready to date yet."

We all settled around the fire with our pizza and talked

about school, and boys, a little bowling, more boys, calculus, the new hit song we couldn't get enough of, and boys.

"I heard Paige cornered you at the football field."

"How did you hear that already?" The memory was enough to take away my appetite.

"Giiirrrl, you're dating Dax DeLeon. Everything you do is being talked about."

"What did she say? Was she her normal snotty self?"

"Pretty much. She said if I didn't break up with Dax, I'd be sorry." I could still see her angry pinched up face as she hissed her warning. My stomach had twisted at her threat. It was a good thing my stargazing date with Dax was coming up. Once he met Dad, I could end this farce. I could take the target off my back and Paige and Gwen could go back to ignoring me.

That thought should have brought me peace of mind. It didn't. Because the idea of not spending time with Dax anymore made my stomach twist even worse than Paige's threat had.

"That girl has some nerve," Rowena said. "Besides, what could she do that she's not already doing? She's already being mean."

"This is Paige were talking about," Bhakti said. "I think she cracked the genetic code on mean."

"That girl serves an all-you-can eat buffet of mean. But you've got Dax, so who cares about her?"

"Yeah, you and Dax. It's pretty exciting. Is he a good kisser?" Gaby asked, and all eyes turned to me.

"Um… I don't know." Yikes! I didn't want to talk about kissing Dax. I didn't even want to think about kissing Dax. Although that hadn't stopped me.

"You mean you and Dax haven't kissed yet? Or you don't know if it's a good kiss?"

"Are you worried that you're a bad kisser?" Rowena asked. "I worry about that too. I mean, how does a girl learn to be a good kisser?"

"My older sister practices by kissing the back of her hand," Bhakti said.

"No. I'm not doing that." I shook my head and laughed. "Honest, everything's fine. The subject of kissing is closed."

"Truth circle time." Rowena moved to sit in the grass.

"What's a truth circle?" I asked as we all joined her on the lawn, holding hands so the circle was complete. "I'll tell you right now, I'm not answering any more questions about kissing Dax."

"It's for team building," Mari said. "We each tell one truth about ourselves that most people don't know."

"We started it at the pizza parties last year as a team bonding exercise," Bhakti said. "Plus, it's fun and sometimes hilarious."

"Yeah it is." Shani laughed. "Ali, you're fresh meat, so you go first."

They already knew my parents were divorced. No way was I going to mention what had happened at my last school. Or how angry I was at my mom. What else did I have? "Um… Oh, I keep a V-log and record something for it almost every day."

"Fun! Is it on YouTube?" Gaby asked.

"Yeah, my private channel. It's not a big deal, just a thing I started after my parents…broke up."

"Oooh, I like that idea," Shani said. "How do you do it? On a computer with a camera?"

"Sometimes. Most of the time I use my phone and upload it to my channel."

Bella nudged her way into the circle, a piece of paper in her mouth, and dropped it onto Mari's lap.

"Aw, she brought me a present!" Mari gave Bella a pat and opened the folded paper. "What did she—"

"Don't open that!" But I was too late. I took a second too long to figure out what it was. Bella had raided my backpack.

"What the heck is this?" Mari frowned down at the note.

"Oh, wow. This can't be right. It's a ransom note."

"What?" Gaby leaned over Mari's shoulder to look as the other girls closed in. "Where did it come from?"

"My backpack."

"You know who took Mr. and Ms. Jackalope?" Rowena asked.

"No! I have no idea."

"Where'd you get this note?" Shani took it from Mari's hand for a closer look.

"It was a mistake! Someone slipped it in my locker, but they think I'm some other girl," I said.

"What do you mean?" Bhakti asked. "Explain."

So I did. I told them about the goons outside of Bowl-O-Rama and *"Where's the playbook?"* and the milkshake. Everything.

"Some girl offered these jerks a football playbook?" Gaby cocked her head. "These guys are trying to cheat."

"Did you tell someone?" Mari asked. "Your dad? Principal Barstow?"

"No. I didn't want to worry my dad over a case of mistaken identity." I'd never forget the pain in his eyes. "And the principal? I couldn't—for a few reasons."

"Like what?" Rowena blinked at me in confusion.

"For one, I never got a good look at them. I have no idea who they are or what they look like. I never even saw their car."

"But you said they were big," Gaby said. "They've got to be football players from a rival school."

"Yeah, but which school? I see the problem," Shani said.

"There's another reason… Seven months ago I lost it. It was after my parents' divorce and things were—not good—and I broke down."

"What do you mean by 'broke down'?" Bhakti asked. "Like an actual mental break down?"

"No, but according to the school psychologist at my old school… Yes," I said. "Things happened and it was bad and kept getting worse. One day I snapped."

"You're one of the calmest, quietest girls at school," Rowena said.

"Not that day I wasn't."

"You're worried they might think you made it up?" Gaby frowned. "You know, like, for attention? Or maybe even that you imagined it?"

"That's what I'm afraid of. Mostly though, is the fact that my dad is finally in a good place. There's no way I want to give him a reason to start worrying about me again."

Shani looked around at all of us nodding. "So, we handle this."

"We? No—you guys don't have to—"

"We're friends, Ali. You can trust us. We've got your back," Mari said.

"Absolutely," Gaby said. "But why do we have to do anything? The fact that they've got the wrong girl doesn't make it Ali's problem."

"The problem is they don't know they have the wrong girl," Shani said. "And now they've got Mr. and Ms. Jackalope."

"We can't let anything happen to those poor rabbits." Mari clenched her napkin in her hand and her eyes teared up. "They need special care. Proper food and enough water. Rabbits can die of fright. A dog bark or loud music can give a rabbit a heart attack."

"I hate to say this but I agree with Mari." Bhakti looked around at us all. "I think we have to make the drop to save Mr. and Ms. Jackalope."

"Meeting them at the bridge and handing over the playbook would get us close enough to see their faces." Shani wiggled her eyebrows up and down. "Then we can find them in a yearbook and turn them in."

"Agreed. But how do we get our hands on the playbook?" Rowena asked. "By tonight?"

All eyes turned to me.

"If only we knew someone dating a football player…" Bhakti tilted her head and raised an eyebrow.

"No. I wouldn't feel right handing them Dax's playbook."

"We can't show up empty-handed," Mari said. "We have to give them the playbook to get the rabbits back."

"We could grab the playbook back as soon as they hand over the rabbits and run."

"Outrun football players? That's not going to happen." Rowena shook her head vigorously.

"Hang on," I said, as the wisp of an idea formed in my head. "What if we didn't hand over 'the' playbook, but gave them 'a' playbook. We can make a fake one."

"I like it." Shani grinned.

"I'll make it! There's a printing shop right down the street from my host family's house." Gaby said. "I love the idea of tricking these jerks."

Me too. Relief swept through my body now that I had a plan to resolve the situation and the fact that I wasn't dealing with it alone.

"Whoa, wait. What about your date with Dax tonight?" Bhakti asked.

"I'll make sure I'm home early." Honestly, it was a good thing. The date was for my dad, not me. Keeping it short and sweet would help me remember that Dax and I weren't real.

"Look at us," Shani said. "Who would have thought our team of nerdy bowlers could be so badass?"

"It actually makes sense." I smiled and couldn't resist. "I mean, we've got balls. Bowling balls."

16

YOU LIED TO MY DAD?

Dax

First Date, Saturday Night, 6:15 p.m.

My phone rang and I smiled seeing "Ali Frost" on my screen. She'd never called me before but I liked it. I liked it a lot. I answered before the second ring.

"Hey, Ali Frost."

"Don't forget you have to come to my door and pick me up for the date. So that my dad can meet you."

"Why wouldn't I?" Did she think I was raised by wolves? No, my Southern mama made sure all her boys knew how to be a gentleman.

"Lots of guys don't. They sit in their car and text from the driveway."

"All your old boyfriends, huh?"

She hesitated before saying, "Sure. Look—remember when you said you owed me one and I said I aimed to collect? This is it."

"All I have to do is ring your doorbell and meet your dad? That's it?"

"That's it."

I shrugged. "I feel like I'm getting off easy."

"After dealing with your ex, I agree."

"Crap, Ali. Has she been bad? We can end this right now if she's being vicious. You don't need to put up with that. I'd hoped she would move on once she saw I was with someone else. It's not like there's a shortage of guys who want to go out with her."

"No, it's okay."

"You let me know when it's not. Deal?"

"Deal."

"Okay. I'll be on your doorstep at seven o'clock."

* * *

I rang Ali's doorbell at six-fifty-nine. Maybe Ali was as anxious as I was because she opened the door right away.

"Hi, Dax."

"You look…" She wore a pair of faded jeans and long-sleeved shirt the exact same shade of green as her eyes.

"Comfortable?" Ali raised an eyebrow at me.

"Well, yeah… But I was going to say pretty."

"Thanks." Her cheeks blushed a soft pink.

"Is your dad here? You know… So I can meet him?"

I heard a loud throat clearing from the room behind Ali as she stepped back to let me in.

"Dad?"

"I'm sitting here reading my magazine." Her father rattled a magazine in front of his face from where he sat in a big leather chair. "Relaxed and cool, that's me. I'm not an overprotective father waiting to grill my daughter's date. Not me. No sir."

"You win father of the year." Ali rolled her eyes at me. "Now please come meet my date."

Ali's dad dropped his magazine and stood.

"Dad, this is—"

"Dax DeLeon. I've seen you play." He stuck his hand out to shake my hand.

"Coach Frost?" What the heck? Ali's dad was Coach Frost? I blinked over at Ali before turning back. "Sir. It's nice to meet you. Again. I met you once before. Sophomore year."

"I remember. You threw three touchdown passes and scored your own rushing touchdown even with a weak offensive line."

"You still beat us."

"We did, but you made us work for it. How's your season going?"

"Good. We're undefeated."

"I know that. I mean, how's *your* season going? Different question."

"Right." I nodded and huffed out a breath. "Not stellar, but..."

"What's Coach Devlin telling you?"

"To get out of my head. To stop overthinking and play for love of the game."

"That's what I would tell you. Devlin's a great coach. You'll work it out," he said. "Where are you two heading?"

"Have you heard of the McDonald Observatory?" I asked.

"Great place. Ali loves going there." Coach Frost smiled. "Don't let me hold you up. You guys have fun."

"Thanks, Dad. I'll be in by two," Ali said, flashing me a grin.

"Good try, kiddo. Midnight sounds good."

"I'll have her back by midnight, Coach Frost. You can count on it," I said.

Ali laughed and steered us out the front door and down her driveway to my truck.

"I can't believe your father is Coach Frost." I opened the passenger door for Ali, shutting it once she was in and buckled. I was still shaking my head when I slid behind the steering wheel. "That's crazy. How did I not put that together?"

"Frost is a fairly common name." She shrugged. "Honestly, I

didn't think about you two knowing about each other either, but the schools are in the same conference so it makes sense."

"Your dad has a pretty big reputation in our part of Texas and the football world." I started my truck and pulled away from the curb. "My girlfriend's father is Coach Frost."

"Your *fake* girlfriend's father is Coach Frost."

"Right. That's what I meant."

"If you don't mind, I'd like to get back closer to eleven-thirty." Ali's gaze darted to me and away quickly. "This is the first time I've gone out in a while—since my parents' divorce actually —and I know my dad will be anxious. I want to make it a little easier on him."

"No problem." And considerate on Ali's part. Plus, I didn't mind looking good in Coach Frost's eyes.

"So, we're going to the McDonald Observatory? I do love that place."

"We're not going to the McDonald Observatory."

"Wait, what? You lied to my dad?"

"I didn't lie. I never said we were going to the Observatory. I asked him if he'd heard of it."

"Maybe not a lie, but misleading. Why in the world—"

"Ali, how do you think your dad would have responded if I told him I was taking his only daughter to one of the darkest places in Texas to lay in the bed of my truck...to stargaze?"

"Oooh, yeah. He wouldn't believe that for a minute."

"Nope." I flashed her a grin. "He's been around teenage boys for too long to trust us."

"We *are* just going to stargaze, aren't we? Because I should let you know my dad taught me a few tricks for boys trying to cop a feel."

"Just stargazing. I imagine we'll talk too, but that's it." I glanced over at her. "You can trust me."

"I'm not great at the trust thing. I don't trust many people."

Rumors had gone around about what had happened over at

Cox and to Coach Frost. Rumors about his daughter which weren't good. Rumors were rarely accurate but either way I couldn't take the look in Ali's eyes.

I pulled over to the curb and stopped my truck. Turning my head, I made sure she could see my face and looked firmly into her eyes.

"Anything that happens between me and a girl—between me and you—will only be mutual. Nothing happens without consent. Period. Full stop. I'm glad your dad taught you how to protect yourself although I hope you'll never have to use it. If I want to kiss you, I'll ask first. Or you could ask." She sighed and relaxed against her seat. "We don't have to go stargazing. I'd be fine grabbing a burger or catching a movie. Or—"

She gently shut me up with a finger over my lips. Her smile made my chest tighten.

"Stargazing works." Her hand slid from my mouth.

"Absolutely. Just stargazing." And because the air between us felt too serious and crisp, I added, "No matter how badly you want me, Ms. Frost, the answer's no."

17

JUST STARGAZING

Dax

Forty-five minutes later—after a detour through the Starbuck's drive-through for hot chocolate—we were stretched out side-by-side in the bed of my truck. I'd thrown two foam pool rafts into the back for comfort and a couple of wool blankets.

We'd been lying there looking for five minutes in complete silence. Because the sky was stunning.

"I don't even know what to say," Ali whispered. "Even in a small town like Devil's Lap, we don't see this. This is…"

"I know. I don't know if there's a word that comes close to describing it."

"It's one thing to know all these stars are out there in the universe. But to see this"—Ali waved her hand at the expansive sky laid open above us—"is mind blowing. This is the starriest and most beautiful sky I've ever seen."

After a long moment of reverent silence at the dazzling sky, we went hunting. I found Orion and the twinkling blue-white Sirius. Ali pointed out Pleiades and Pegasus off to the east.

Together we found the Milky Way and argued over which was Polaris, the North Star. It was hard to pick the brightest star when an infinity of stars and constellations spread out forever in every direction. Once we'd picked out all the stars and constellations we knew, we lay for a while in quiet appreciation.

"This might have the McDonald Observatory beat." She wiggled next to me on the foam mat, settling in more. "When I look through the telescope at the observatory it's amazing but distant. The stars are off far away in space. Out here—lying under this—it's like I can reach out and grab one. Like I'm part of this whole dazzling sky."

"Like we're just another bright speck of light suspended inside in a constellation."

"Yes. Exactly like that."

I turned my head toward her. "Would you have guessed that day we met in the counseling office that we'd have so much in common?"

"Heck no." A giggle escaped her lips before she slapped a hand over her mouth to smother it.

"What's so funny?"

"I sort of thought you were a douche-canoe."

"Hey now." I reached out and tickled along her ribs.

"Stop," she said, laughter in her voice. "I have since revised that opinion."

"Good," I said, turning back to the stars. "I, on the other hand, was totally intrigued by you that day."

"I guess that explains why you added the bowling class."

"Absolutely. Can I ask you a question?" Now that I knew who Ali was, I needed to know if the rumors about Coach Frost's daughter were true.

"Not if it's about kissing."

"It's not." Not at all. Sure, I'd thought about kissing Ali. But only when we'd discussed it as a "couple" thing. Okay, maybe one or two more times after that. It hadn't been on my list of the top five things I needed to survive. Until right now. Which, where the heck had that come from? Ali rolled her head toward me. The darkness made it hard to read the emotion on her face. "Not yet anyway."

"What do you want to know?"

"What happened at your old high school? There were rumors that Coach Frost got divorced and quit coaching before the end of last season."

Ali released a sigh that cut through the cool, quiet night. "My mom had an affair with the assistant football coach. You know, my dad's assistant coach. Dad had no idea and neither did I. Not a clue. If there had been rumors floating around, we hadn't heard them."

Oh, man.

"A student walked in on them." She paused for a moment, sucking in a shaky breath. "It was shocking and painful and ugly. There was no escape from the sordid details flying around school. It was like running from a swarm of killer bees we couldn't shake."

"Wow. That had to be awful."

"It was. It was bad. And then it got worse."

"You mean the divorce?"

"That. Definitely that. But also, the fallout. Dad and I tried to pick up the pieces and keep going. Even though my mom and the assistant coach were moved to another school district right away, I still had school and dad still had the football team the coach.

"I tried. I really tried to keep it together, but I was just so devastated. And angry—so, so angry at my mom. I cried a lot. Lost weight. Just sort of shut down."

She got quiet and the silence dragged on.

I should have let it go right there. But I needed to know one more thing.

"Is it true you tried to commit suicide? After your parents' divorce?"

"*What?* No. God no." She stiffened up next to me and shook her head. "Stupid rumors."

"What did happen? I mean, if you're okay talking about it."

"What happened was my dad was seriously worried about me. So he quit. He resigned as the football coach. Three weeks before football playoffs, he quit to focus on me."

"Man, I knew Cox had lost all their coaches suddenly, but... Wow. We live and breathe football here in Texas. Trust me, I know. That couldn't have been easy."

"It wasn't fun. That's when the notes started. It was my fault Cox's winningest football coach quit. My fault Cox didn't make it to the state championship for the first time in six years. My fault two of Cox's star players didn't get to set playoff records."

"That's bullshit. It wasn't your fault."

"That's not how every student at Cox saw it."

"You didn't tell anyone about the notes? Not even your friends?"

"Ha! What friends? The friends I thought I had turned on me too."

"That sucks. That totally sucks." I reached out and took Ali's hand in mine.

"I put up with the notes, the whispers, and the names for four months. Then one day...I couldn't. I was at my locker swapping out my books between classes... And there was another note. I lost it." She turned her face back up to the sky. "I screamed, cried, tossed my books out of my locker all over the hallway."

"What happened after the meltdown?"

"When I finally stopped acting like a raging, rabid dog, I took the stack of notes from my locker and marched them down to the principal's office. I guess someone had already called my dad because he was there. They only made it through half of the stack of notes when Principal Vale suggested I transfer schools. I transferred to Jackson the next day."

"It's weird. While you were going through hell—I was in football heaven. We beat your old school to make it into the championship game, and it only happened because your dad had quit. Because of your pain. We had never beaten Cox before. Your dad was too good of a coach."

"You're welcome."

"I'd give it all back if it meant saving you from all of that."

Ali blinked into my face, searching my eyes.

"I think you actually mean that," she whispered.

"I do." I turned fully on my side toward her.

"I lost everyone." She faced the sky again. "Everyone I loved and trusted. Everyone except my dad. I felt betrayed, isolated, and angry. But more than anything, I hurt. Between my mom, my friends, and watching my dad's pain, my heart broke."

"Ali?"

She turned her face toward me. "Yes?"

"One more question…"

"I think that's everything."

"Not quite. Because now I'm asking…would you mind if I kissed you?"

She rolled onto her side, putting us face to face. "Is this because you feel sorry for me? I don't think I could stand a pity kiss."

"Not pity." I pulled in a breath of cool, crisp air. "That's not to say I don't feel bad about what you and your dad went through. I do. But if all of that crap hadn't gone down, you and I might never have met. That would have been my loss."

"Mine too," Ali whispered and leaned into me.

Into our first kiss. Nothing crazy. Nothing wild. Just her lips against mine. And it was the best kiss I'd ever had. Slowly, I pulled back an inch. "Was that okay?"

"That was perfect." She rolled back, her face to the stars and a smile on her lips.

I rolled back too, face to the sky. Lying here next to Ali...it felt like the universe got something right. I reached my hand over and found hers, interlocked our fingers and held tight.

18

DO YOU THINK WE'RE STUPID?

Ali

Dax had me back home by eleven-thirty and insisted on walking me to the door. If you're wondering if Dax kissed me goodnight, the answer is...sort of. He stood close, his deep, dark eyes hot on my lips. Then he pulled me in even closer, pressed a kiss on my temple, and whispered, "That's in case your dad is watching."

After saying goodnight to my dad, I went to my room planning to spend the next fifteen minutes replaying both kisses through my head on an endless loop while listening to my dad go through his lock up the house routine.

I'd been telling myself for weeks now that this thing between me and Dax wasn't real. But that kiss under the stars felt very, very real. Real to me. It was time to face the truth.

I liked Dax DeLeon.

Was it possible Dax and I could go from fake to fact? Did he like me too or was he that great an actor? Could I even trust enough to let someone close to me again? Or had that already happened? With my teammates—now my friends. With Dax—now my... Well, that was still to be determined.

I trusted him enough to open up and tell him all the ugly details of the last year. So maybe—

A light tap on my window startled me. I whipped around and—speak of the devil—it was Dax.

Crossing the room to the window, I slid it open. "What are you doing here?"

"I forgot I wanted to ask you one more question," he said, his voice a hushed tone. Luckily my dad's bedroom was on the opposite side of the house.

"What?"

"Will you go to the winter dance with me?"

My pulse fluttered. "The one in two weeks?"

"Yes."

Wait. Calm down. This isn't about me. "This is part of the fake relation—"

"No. It's not. I realized over a week ago, that whenever we're together—I'm not faking anymore. I'm not sure I ever was. I like you, Ali Frost. I'd like us to go to the dance as a real couple. Would you please put me out of my misery and say yes?"

"Yes."

He smiled his crooked smile at me. "Would it be all right if I kiss you again?"

"Yes. It would be more than all right."

Dax leaned in, cupped my jaw with one hand, and kissed me. Kissed me breathless. And then he was gone.

Wow. Well, that settled that. Dax DeLeon liked me too.

For the next ten minutes I paced my room, anxious to get the whole rabbit rescue over with. At precisely ten minutes before midnight, I snuck out of my bedroom window and down half a block to where Bhakti's van was waiting for me.

Was *supposed* to be waiting for me. Bhakti's van wasn't there. Something dark and jagged clawed at me. Doubt seeped in through those exposed spaces. *You can trust us.* Apparently, my new friends were no different from my old friends.

Wait. No. That wasn't fair. This was different. Just because they decided not to come—that was nothing like what my old friends had done. Honestly, I couldn't blame my teammates for backing out. There was no reason for them to risk getting in trouble. Not for me.

I could do this alone. I should do this alone and leave them out of it. I turned to walk home for my car when headlights cut through the darkness behind me.

Bhakti pulled up to the curb and warmth blossomed in my chest.

The side door slid open and Rowena and Shani pulled me in and we were off, heading for Old Devil's Bridge.

"Sorry we're late," Shani said. "I forgot what time we'd agreed to. Ro was scared we'll get in trouble so it took a few minutes to calm her down, and then Bhakti couldn't decide if she should turn right or left on Porter Street."

"You guys know I have trouble making decisions. Someone else should have driven," Bhakti said, her gaze bouncing from the road, to the rearview mirror, to the side mirror and back to the road again.

"We're good. We're not late. Everyone ready?" I asked, looking around at their faces in the shadowy van. "Do you have the playbook, Gaby?"

"Yep." She patted the book in her lap. "It looks real too."

"Hey, how was your date with Dax?" Mari asked.

"Pretty great." I was glad no one could see me blush. "He, um, asked me to the winter dance."

The girls squealed their excitement.

"You have to take us shopping," Shani said. "No way are you picking your dress without us."

"Deal. Dresses aren't my thing, so I'll be glad for the help."

"You guys, we're here." Bhakti turned onto Devil's Bridge

Road and slowed the van to a crawl, making a U-turn before parking. "I want to be ready for our quick getaway."

Kids called Old Devil's Bridge the bridge to nowhere since the road ended up at a dead end at a long-ago abandoned oil rig. There were no street lights or nearby neighborhoods, so it was also a popular make-out spot. Rumored to be. I had no actual knowledge about that.

"No other car or truck yet," Rowena said. "You guys, I'm so scared I might pee myself."

"I'm nervous too," Bhakti said. "It feels like there's a hummingbird flying around in my chest."

"Stay calm, everyone." Shani gave me a nod. "Ali, go over the plan again, so we're all straight."

"Right. Gaby, you hand over the playbook at the same time I grab the rabbit cage."

"Got it," Gaby said.

"Ro and Shani, you two memorize the make, model and plates of their vehicle."

Rowena and Shani fist bumped.

"Bhakti and Mari are going to get a good look at their faces so we can identify them and turn them in."

"They're still not here. Maybe they won't show up." Mari glanced back at the bridge. "Whoa, wait. They're here. Standing on the bridge. It's pretty dark, but I think I see the cage with them."

"No car? No truck?" Bhakti shook her head. "No license plate. Our plan is already messed up."

"You guys don't have to do this," I said. "I can—"

"Shut up, Ali," Shani said. "We're doing this. We're all doing this together."

We exited the van and walked in a line toward the figures on the bridge. When we got in range to see their faces our plan took another hit.

"Dang it," Rowena whispered. "Ski masks. There goes identifying the goons."

"It's okay," I whispered back. "We'll still walk away with the rabbits. That's all we really need."

We stopped ten feet away from them.

"Hey," Goon #1 said. "You were supposed to come alone."

"Yeah, I ignored that." I shrugged. "Now, are we doing this, or what? We don't have all night to stand around and chit chat."

"Hand over the playbook." Goon #2 held out his beefy hand. "Then you'll get the stupid rabbits."

Gaby stepped forward, about to hand over the playbook, when I grabbed her and pulled her back.

"First, shine a light on the cage so we can see the rabbits." I crossed my arms over my chest trying to look tough and steely-eyed but it also hid my shaking hands.

One of them clicked on a small flashlight and aimed it at the cage while the other lifted the sheet up for us to see.

"Oh, thank goodness," Mari said. "You two jerks are lucky they're okay."

"Zip it," Goon #1 growled. "Now let me see the playbook."

"No." I shook my head. "We hand off at the same time."

"Whatever. Just give it to us already." He picked up the cage by the two side handles and waited.

Gaby and I stepped forward. I wrapped both of my hands as tight as I could around the handle on top of the cage and gave Gaby a nod. She handed over the playbook at the same time I grabbed the cage and pulled.

The cage didn't budge. It went nowhere. Duh. If the huge, hulking goon wasn't ready to let go—it wasn't going anywhere.

"Do you think we're stupid?" my goon said, holding tight to the cage while Gaby's goon flipped through the playbook.

"Yes," I said.

"What the hell?" the other goon snarled. Seriously, it was a snarl. "You guys must think we're stupid. Or did you think this was funny? You're going to regret this."

The guy ripped the cage from my hands and the two took off into some scrub pines. Then before we could follow, engines coughed to life and two dirt bikes, one with the rabbit cage perched precariously on the handle bars, shot past us and disappeared in a cloud of dirt.

"What is their problem?" Shani stood with her hands on her hips staring into the darkness they'd ridden off into. "Why did those jerks get so pissy?"

Bhakti picked the playbook up off the ground and leafed through it with the light of her phone. "Because Gaby's from Argentina—where football is—"

"Soccer! Lo sabia! I knew that! I knew that! Que soy una idiota." Gaby held both hands to her head and groaned. "I was so fired up, I didn't think. I'm so sorry."

Soccer. Right. I hadn't even thought of that.

"Complete utter failure," Rowena grumbled.

"We found out Mr. and Ms. Jackalope are alive," Mari said. "That's a good thing."

You know what sounded like a good thing right now?

Flying to Argentina and escaping this whole stupid, idiotic mess.

19

BOWLING DOESN'T HAVE
CHEERLEADERS

DAX

BOWLING CLASS, FRIDAY NOV 8, 8:10 A.M.

The more I got to know Ali the more I liked her. I hoped she felt
the same way about me. Sometimes I wasn't sure. Most of the
time we spent together was relaxed and comfortable, but there
were a few times when Ali acted uneasy. Nervous even.

It could have been because we did this whole thing back-
wards. Were together—pretending at least—before we got to
know each other. Before we both decided it was the real thing.
Or it could be because being with me put her in the spotlight. I
understood that. After everything she went through at her last
school, knowing how cruel some kids could be, I got how that
would make her anxious. My hope was that her nervousness
would smooth out and disappear when she realized that it
wasn't going to happen again. Not on my watch.

Today was "A" day, which meant bowling class with Ali.
Between my football schedule and Ali's bowling schedule this
class was some of our best time together.

"All right, Dax," Ali said after picking up her spare. "Your turn. See if you can beat that, hotshot."

"Oh, I'll try." I hardly ever beat her and I didn't care. It was a fun competition though. It didn't hurt that Ali gave me tips on bowling form and technique. Thanks to her, my game was improving. I took my position on the apron and rolled. Sometimes I was lucky and sheer power made up for my lack of technique. This was one of those times. "Strike. How do you like that?"

"I bow to your bowling skills. You won this round." Ali stood to take her turn, adjusting her ball in her grip. She was halfway through her five-step roll when Paige interrupted.

"Looks like we'll be competing against each other, Frosty."

Ali's hand jerked on the release and she threw the first gutter ball I'd seen her roll.

"Oh, no! Did I mess you up? My bad." Paige didn't look sorry at all. She looked...like someone who held a good poker hand.

"What are you talking about?"

"She's talking about the winter dance. Someone nominated you for Ms. Jackalope." Ali looked horrified at that. Which would have made me laugh if I didn't understand why she hated being the center of attention. I could kick myself for not thinking to mention it on the bus ride here so Paige wasn't the one to give her the news.

"Why would they do that?" Ali shook her head.

"Right?" Gwen snorted. "I guess dating Dax was your ticket to fame."

No. I knew why kids would nominate her. Now that everyone had finally noticed her, they could see how smart, pretty, talented, and nice she was.

"Good luck, Ali." Paige wore a cool, confident smile in the next lane. "I mean it's all good fun. Remember when we were crowned last year, Dax?"

Ali jumped up from her chair. "I'm going—um, to say hello to Mr. J. I'll be back."

This was the third time Ali had left our lane today. Pretty sure Ali's breaks were the only thing keeping her from dropping a bowling ball on Paige's foot to shut her up.

"Old news," I said, picking up my ball to take my turn and block Paige out. My first roll resulted in a 7-10 split. I missed a spare on my second roll by only knocking down the 7 pin.

"Hey, Dax, is this Ali's phone?" Paige asked. "Found it on the ground. I guess she dropped it."

"Yeah, it's hers." I took it and slid it into the side pocket on Ali's backpack.

"You should let her down gently," Paige said. "She doesn't have a shot at Ms. Jackalope and I'd hate for her to get her hopes up."

"I'll get right on that." Night and day these two. I chuckled imagining the look on Ali's face if she won. Probably the same face she'd make if a big fat hairy spider dropped in front of her.

Ali returned, sliding into the chair next to me and checking out my score. "Tut, tut, Mr. DeLeon. Tell your bowling coach you need work on your spares."

"My coach is busy with her own bowling game," I said. "Speaking of, I wish I could make it to watch your competition today but there's no way with the regional playoff game tomorrow."

"I understand. No big deal." Ali shrugged.

"Bowling competitions? I didn't even know they had those." Gwen's face scrunched up like she'd caught a whiff of skunk. "It's not like it's an actual sport. I mean, they don't even have cheerleaders."

"It's a sport." I threw a glance over at Paige and Gwen before turning back to Ali. "Ali happens to be one of the top five players in the state of Texas. She's made the all-state team two years in a row, and even set a record for highest three-game score in a meet."

Ali blinked at me in surprise. "How did you even know that?"

"Your dad bragged a little the last time I dropped you off." I was glad he had, otherwise I might not have known. Ali sure didn't mention it. "I was dang impressed, so I did some research."

"But it's bowling," Paige said. "Who actually cares?"

"I care. And it turns out some schools offer scholarships to the top bowlers." I'd come a long way from not knowing we even had a bowling team.

Ali smiled at me and there went that tug in my chest again.

"What I was trying to say before we were interrupted"—I turned my back on Paige and Gwen, hoping they'd take the hint —"was we've got a bye week next week so I can make it to your meet next Friday."

Ali's eyes went wide before she sent me a tentative smile. "I'd like that."

On the ride back to school, Ali and I sat together—something we'd started right after we became a "couple"—in the seat behind the bus driver.

"So, Ali, about Mr. and Ms. Jackalope…"

"What?" Ali jumped like I'd popped a balloon next to her, taking her by surprise. "I don't know anything about them. Are they still missing? Do you know who took them? Or… I mean… What about them?"

"I have no idea who took them. I'm talking about the nomination for Mr. and Ms. Jackalope for the dance," I clarified.

"Oh, right. That. What about it?"

"I wanted to give you a heads up. Every nominee has to make a short video about why they should be crowned."

She frowned at me. "What if I don't want to be crowned?"

"It's just for fun. That's all." I wrapped my arm around her shoulders. "Fun and school spirit. Speaking of fun and school spirit, are you still coming to the game tomorrow night?"

"I'll be there."

"Good. Will you wait for me after the game?"

"So Paige can see us together. Sure."

"No. For me."

* * *

Friday's game was almost a repeat of the week before. First half we were clicking. Everything worked. My passes were dead-on accurate, our receivers looked like they had glue on their hands, and our defense worked overtime keeping the other team from scoring.

It only took one blip in the third quarter to land me in quicksand. It was the bomb pass to TJ that sent a twinge through my shoulder. Not bad, but enough to start a chain reaction. A flash of doubt led to a hesitation. That hesitation—even just a fraction of a second—threw off my timing. No interception this time, but the momentum swung to the other team.

"DeLeon, come off!" Coach Devlin called from the sidelines. "Murph, you're in."

Murph. Our back-up quarterback.

I jogged off the field to the sidelines, "Coach—"

"Murph needs some playing time." He tucked his clipboard under his arm. "Take a breather. Clear your head. You'll be back in fourth quarter."

Clear my head. Oh, yeah. I needed to clear my head of the rabbit hole of negative thinking.

Embrace the suck and move on. One bad possession. One bad throw. That's all it was. Focus on the now. On what I could control. My thoughts. Positive thoughts. I'd find my receivers and throw. Stay focused on the moment. Receivers, throw.

Receivers, throw. No hesitation. I'd trust my accuracy and my receiver's talent.

I went back in for the fourth quarter with the score tied. Maybe Coach was trying to prop up my confidence because he called mostly rushing plays. We easily scored one rushing touchdown, scored on a fumble recovery, and capped it off with a field goal to win the game.

Everyone was pretty stoked in the locker room after the game. Laughing and bragging. I knew I had nothing to brag about. I stood feeling like an imposter who'd snuck onto the field. Coach had pulled me out of the game. That hadn't happened to me since I was a sophomore.

"You heading to the lake?" TJ asked.

"Maybe." I didn't want to commit before I ran it by Ali. Hanging out with Paige and her friends probably wasn't on Ali's top one million things she'd like to do list. "Ali and I are going to grab something to eat first."

"Come on, DeLeon." Josh leaned on TJ's shoulder. "We need you there, man, to celebrate the win."

"Pretty sure you can handle it without me." I gave him my serious captain of the football team look. "In case I don't make it, don't do anything stupid."

Turned out, Ali was okay with the bonfire at the lake. On the condition that we bailed when her Paige-limit had been reached. Worked for me.

In no time we were sitting around a roaring bonfire, on a downed river oak, with our bag of burgers and fries between us. It was cool watching Ali get along with my friends. TJ and Grady, my closest friends, accepted her easily into our circle.

Most of the kids did. With a few exceptions.

"Gosh, Frost, we've never had a bowler infiltrate our bonfire before." Paige's eyes glittered across the fire.

Infiltrate. Like Ali was the enemy.

Turned out, I reached my Paige-limit before Ali did.

I stood, pulling Ali up with me, and gave TJ a nod before heading to my truck. Sure, we could have put up with Paige, but why bother? Ali could hold her own, but I wasn't going to sit and watch Paige treat her like her own personal tackling dummy.

2 0

FRONT PORCH SITTING

Dax

I drove us to Ali's house from the bonfire since it was pretty late. I pulled up at the curb in front of her house and shut off the engine.

"Okay if we sit on your porch for a bit?" I glanced at her house, seeing the glow of light in the family room. Overprotective dad alert. "If we stay in my truck, your dad might think—"

"He totally might." She grinned across at my predicament. "Say no more. Front porch it is."

"I do *not* want to get on your dad's bad side."

She laughed as she sat on the swing, her feet up, hugging her legs to her chest and resting her chin on her knees. "Yeah, I've heard that a lot from guys."

"Your dad sort of walks on water in the football world." I sat, angling my back against the arm so I could see Ali's face and pushed off with one foot, sending us into a gentle swing. "Do you think he'll go back to coaching?"

"I hope so."

"As the daughter of a coach, I'm guessing you practically grew up on the sidelines and know football as well as I do."

"I know a few things about football," she said.

"What did you think of the game tonight?" I asked. "Honest opinion."

"I'm not sure what you're looking for here... Personally, when it comes to my bowling, I like when my dad or Coach gives it to me straight." She sent me a guarded glance. "Platitudes and praise? Or the straight deal?"

"Straight deal," I said. "I can take it."

"Okay. Well, I thought you had an excellent first half. Some amazing passes. I can see why the scouts are interested." She sucked in a breath and looked directly in my eyes. "Your third quarter was shaky. You seemed to lose your rhythm. I don't know—you looked tentative. Something was off. It created an opening for their defense which made you rush your passes and miss your receivers."

I turned my head, staring off into the darkness and it got quiet between us with only the sound of a screech owl and soft rustling leaves to break the silence. I sliced a hand through my hair and huffed out a breath.

"Hey..." she started, reaching out and touching the back of my hand lightly.

"Yep." I nodded and looked back at her, a half smile sliding over my face. "I was hoping Coach Frost's daughter would give it to me straight and you did. I stunk on ice in the second half."

"You didn't stink." She wrapped her hand around mine with a squeeze. "What happened in the third quarter?"

"I don't know. Overthinking. Negative thoughts. Second guessing. Pick one," I said, running my free hand across the back of my neck. "I've created my own boogey man and I can't shake him."

"Have you tried working with a sports psychologist?" She shrugged. "A lot of high school athletes do now."

"Yeah. I've got techniques to depressurize." Ways to stop negative thinking. To let go of a bad play and move on. "It's just lately they don't always work."

"I'm going to go Nana Frost on you. When I had a problem I couldn't solve, she used to ask me one question and it helped me put things in perspective." She sat up, one knee still curled under her but she'd dropped her other leg down to tangle with mine. "What's the worst that could happen if you don't find a solution?"

"The worst? College recruiters will lose interest." My dream would be over. Heck, even thinking about the possibility made my stomach clench. "So pretty much the end of football for me."

"And?" She blinked up at me like she wasn't getting it.

"And? You don't understand—I'm saying no more football. Football is my life. It's who I am. I'm a football player."

"Maybe I'm the only one who *does* understand. I don't put you on a pedestal like a lot of kids at school. Heck, even some teachers and parents give you special treatment. I can see how easy it is to get wrapped up in the star quarterback role. But you're more than a football player." Now it was her turn to look away, her face serious, like she was deciding if she should say something or not. She turned back, a small smile on her lips. "You don't have to prove yourself out on that field. Not to me. A loss doesn't dent your armor. You aren't just a jock. You're smart and nice and funny. You're a great guy who happens to play football."

"I get what you're saying, but I don't know that guy."

"I do. I know that guy. I think deep down you do too. Only you don't trust that guy. You don't trust who you are when you aren't on the football field."

Was Ali right? It was true I'd been admired for my football skills since middle school. Everywhere I went when people met me it was always connected to football. *You're the kid with the*

great arm. You could win the Heisman, son. Hey, aren't you the quar-
terback who set that passing record. What was I without football?

"Here's another thought," Ali said. "Maybe that's your problem on the field too. You don't trust yourself."

21

BAD LUCK AND BIG FOOT

Ali

LUNCH, MONDAY NOV 11

"No, it's true. I heard Josh Radnor tell Sofia González. According to Josh we almost lost the game all because Mr. and Ms. Jackalope weren't there. They always bring the team good luck." This was from Ashley, another cheerleader, sitting next to Gwen at the lunch table. "Remember last year when they missed two games because of an ear infection? We lost both of those games."

I didn't believe in lucky mascots myself but the fact that the rabbits were still missing had me squirming in my seat. I shouldn't feel guilty because two football players had belly-button lint where their brains should be and mistakenly roped me into their scheme.

"Is it true Dax? TJ?" Paige leaned forward across from Dax, her forehead creased with worry. "Is the team cursed with bad luck until the mascots are back?"

I dumped my lunch from the brown bag, trying to tune out the bunny conversation.

"No the team isn't cursed." Dax looked at his tray of food without enthusiasm. "Man, I wish every day was Wednesday. I think Kev's menu has spoiled me."

"You aren't kidding. Bhakti Patel's mom's curry last week was banging," TJ said.

I swallowed down a bite of my peanut butter, jelly, and ranch potato chip sandwich which was not banging. Ugh. How did my dad think this was a good combination?

"Well, that's not what Josh said," Gwen added.

"When did Josh become an expert on curry?" Grady asked.

"Not curry, silly." Gwen did some pouty lip thing in Grady's direction. "I'm talking about what Josh said about the bad luck."

"Josh also thinks Bigfoot is real," Dax said.

TJ nodded. "Luck has nothing to do with whether we win or lose."

I handed my Twinkie over to Dax. "Could you pass this down to Kev?"

He smiled and the Twinkie was passed down the table to a happy Kev. Although, he was already happy. The Twinkie just was icing on the happy cake.

"Awww, no banana note from daddy today?" Gwen asked, but I think everyone knew it wasn't a question.

"Nope." I held up my orange so she could see today's message blazoned in black Sharpie before reading it out loud. "'Orange you glad I didn't write your note on a banana? xo Dad.'"

TJ laughed—with me, I thought, not *at* me.

"Ha!" Dax gave me his crooked smile. "I love your dad."

* * *

That afternoon we lost another team competition. Coach gave us her barracuda/goldfish speech again. Pretty sure that was at least the fiftieth time we'd heard that speech. You'd think Coach would figure out it wasn't working.

We headed out to the parking lot together—something we started doing ever since the goons had jumped me—feeling frustrated at coming up short again.

"I'm sorry, y'all. This time it was my fault," Shani said. "I rolled that gutter ball when we needed a spare."

"No. It was me." Bhakti patted her chest, taking ownership of the team loss. "I didn't have a single strike today. I might as well have bowled blindfolded."

Gaby sighed loudly. "I lost it for us. I had my worst game ever today."

"I choked," Rowena said. "I always do. I can't take the pressure. I let Kayla get in my head. Between her gold bowling shoes and her smack talk, I couldn't focus."

"Ugh. Kayla Tercera." Mari snorted. "Who wears shiny gold bowling shoes anyway?"

"Snotty bowlers who think they're all that," Shani grumbled.

"It wasn't any single person's fault," I said. "I had a bad game too."

"But your bad game is still better than all of ours." Bhakti stopped in front of her van which was parked next to mine, another thing we made sure to do now. "Looks like someone put trash on your hood, Ali. I bet it was Tercera. That girl was pissed you beat her in the individual competition."

"I agree. She talked a lot of smack, but turned into a whiny baby when she lost." Shani leaned forward to grab the trash, but pulled her hand back with a yelp. "Oh, gross! It's a rabbit's foot. A bloody rabbit's foot!"

"How could they do that?" Mari's voice wobbled on the edge of tears. "Those poor rabbits!"

"Jerks," Gaby said.

Rowena leaned forward, adjusting her glasses. "There's a note under it."

"Gross." This time Mari actually gagged. "I'm not touching it."

I moved around to the driver's side of the hood for a better look. "Wait. That's not a real rabbit's foot. It's one of those dumb key chains."

"And not blood." Bhakti nodded to an empty ketchup packet tossed on the pavement next to my car.

Shani grabbed the note and read it out loud, "Next time real deal. Bring the Playbook! Coyote Tom's Drive-in. Park in Spot P-7. Friday 11:30 night."

"These guys are pissing me off."

"I hate to say this, Ali, but I think we need to give them the real playbook to save the rabbits and put an end to this."

I didn't see any other way either. Nothing had changed since the last time we'd had to deal with these goons. We still had no way to identify them. My school still thought I might be a mental case. (I doubted it was an accident that Dr. Boyd managed to pop his head into one of my classes once a week.) I was absolutely not going to have my dad start worrying about me all over again.

"Before I do this, is everyone sure you don't know a player on the team?" Because I really, really didn't want to steal Dax's playbook.

"I wish," Shani said.

"Sorry, no." Gaby shook her head along with the other girls.

"Okay then." I sucked in a breath and nodded. I had to focus on getting the rabbits back. Then I could worry about Dax and my guilty conscience.

Steal the playbook. Save the rabbits.

2 2
PDA AT A BOWLING MEET

Dax

ALI'S BOWLING MEET, FRIDAY NOV 15, 4:30 P.M.

Friday after school I drove to Spare & Strike in the next town over to watch Ali bowl. I stood back, leaning against the half wall behind the lanes not wanting to distract her and risk getting her in trouble with Coach again. At one point our eyes met and she gave me a nod, but that was it. She was in the zone. I knew a couple girls on the team. Shani and I had been in the same elementary school and often in the same class. Bhakti and I had been lab partners in seventh grade earth science.

Watching Ali compete was both what I expected and a complete surprise. The expected? How cool she was under pressure. Just like in class she had a way of locking out the world around her and hyper-focusing on each roll.

What was surprising was how vocal she was when it wasn't her turn. She called out encouragement to the girls on her team. She grabbed their hands, looked them in the eyes, and settled their nerves. Her teammates went to her for advice on shots as much as they went to Coach Diamond. The girls fist bumped, high fived, and cheered each other on.

After watching for almost two hours I knew two things: Ali was phenomenal. Their team, not so much. They were missing that killer instinct that made good players great competitors. In my experience, from years playing football and lacrosse, that killer instinct was innate and almost impossible to teach.

When the scores were tallied at the end, Ali won the individual girl's division (setting a high score even) but the Jackson Jackalopes lost the team competition. I listened to Coach's postgame wrap-up. One of those standard coach critiques that covered the good, the bad, and what to fix for next time. Somehow that involved fish. They finished with a team cheer.

It was only then that Ali turned her attention my way.

"That was some impressive bowling," I said.

"Thanks." She placed her ball in her bag and sat to change shoes. "But you see me bowl in class."

"Turns out it's not the same. I thought you had amazing focus in class, but you have nerves of steel." Her game face was fierce which I found seriously hot.

"I've had a lot of practice the last year." She shoved her shoes in her bag too and stood. "Shutting everything out was the only way I survived most days."

I hated that she'd gone through that, but her strength amazed me. I closed the distance between us and kissed her. A simple brush of my lips against hers. Not really a kiss but communication. A message. Of support. Of respect. Of—okay, yeah, it was a kiss too. No denying it; my heartbeat shot from a jog to a sprint at the touch of her lips.

When I pulled back not only did Ali look a bit flustered and breathless, but so did her teammates who were loosely gathered around us in a semicircle.

"PDA at a bowling meet?" Bhakti grinned and shook her head. "Never saw that coming."

"Uh…great bowling out there, ladies," I said.

"Thanks," Shani said.

Coach startled me with a slap on the shoulder.

"Nice to see you come out and support your fellow Jack-alopes, DeLeon," she said.

"Yes, ma'am. It was fun to watch."

"Fun?" Coach shook her head and swung her gaze around the team. "Hear that? No. I want you girls to dig deep and find that killer instinct. I want people to watch you bowl and swear they were witnesses to a crime because of the way you dispatched your opponents. I want other teams to shake in their bowling shoes when they see the Jackson Jackalopes on their schedule."

Whoa.

Coach wandered off mumbling something about the snack bar.

"Are you ready to go?" I asked Ali. "I can follow you to your house so we can drop off your car before we go eat."

"I didn't drive. I caught a ride with Shani."

"Smart thinking." I nodded to all the girls.

Ali grabbed her bag before turning to her teammates. "G'night."

"We'll see you later," Rowena said, then grunted when Shani elbowed her.

"She didn't mean later tonight," Bhakti said. "Because later you'll be out with Dax. So, of course, not later tonight."

"Later this weekend," Gaby said.

"Or later at school," Mari added. "On Monday."

With one more wave from Ali to her friends, we headed out to the parking lot.

"What was that about?" I gave a jerk of my head back toward the building.

"That?" Ali blinked and shrugged. "Maybe you make them nervous. That whole star football player effect."

Ah, yeah. It happened sometimes. I still found it strange, but this was Texas where football was like oxygen.

"Hold on a sec." I unlocked my truck, pulled open the passenger door, and flipped the seat forward. Ali handed me her bowling bag and I shoved it in next to my athletic bag rather than have it slide around the bed of the truck. "All set."

We settled in and buckled up. "Burger or pizza?"

"A burger and a banana milkshake sound perfect."

I didn't care what we ate. Spending time with Ali sounded like a perfect Friday night.

We met up with TJ at Burger Barn. The crazy thing was Ali had just set a new record for the highest 2-game score in the district and yet all the attention was on me when we walked in. *Great game last week, Dax! Good luck in the playoffs! We need a win, DeLeon!*

After going through the line to get our food, we joined TJ at the booth he'd grabbed.

"Ali, this is my friend Shay."

"Hi," Ali said, scooting into the booth to make room for me.

"How's it going, Shay?" Shay and TJ had grown up next door to each other, although she'd been homeschooled ever since a bad accident in fourth grade—one that left scarring on one side of her face. Her parents insisted she attend Jackson this year to prepare her for college. Her long hair fell forward, covering one side of her face like a protective curtain, but a shy smile peeped out in greeting.

We ate and talked. Ali and Shay seemed to hit it off, finding some common ground to talk about. They even did that girl trip to the bathroom together. While they were gone our talk turned to next week's game. And girls. Always girls, right?

"Maybe I'm wrong," TJ said. "But your pretend thing with Ali sure looks pretty real."

I dropped my gaze down to my soda before meeting his eyes again. "Look, I know I said no relationships this year. But—"

"Hey, I'm not knocking it. I like her. Much better than your last girlfriend," TJ said. "As long as you stay focused and help us win games."

"That's the plan." TJ was my best friend, but I hadn't told him about the pressure I was feeling on the field. How it was messing with my head and throwing me off my game. The last thing our team needed was to lose faith in me. Sometimes confidence was the edge in a closely fought game. "Speaking of girlfriends… Are you and Shay together?"

"No." It was his turn to avoid eye contact. He shook his head firmly and looked back at me with a frown. "We're just friends is all."

"Uh huh." The more he frowned across at me the bigger my smile grew. This would explain why TJ never seemed interested in the girls who flirted with him. He was crushing on his neighbor. "For what it's worth, I like her."

"I told you it's not like that," he grumbled.

The girls arrived back at the table and he shot me a warning glance.

Instead of sliding back into the booth, Ali held out her hand and asked, "Can I have the truck keys? I want to go grab something from my bag."

"I can grab it for you."

"No! I mean, you stay. I'll get it." She placed her hand on my shoulder which I liked a lot. "It'll only take me a second."

Girl stuff. I pulled the keys from my pocket and handed them over. "Sure."

Ali looked at the keys in her hand like I'd handed her a tarantula. Then she nodded, wrapped her hand around them, and gave me a stiff smile. "Be right back."

She left, moving quickly to the door and out. Nervous again. I glanced around the place, looking for Paige or one of her friends. Or maybe she'd run into someone in the bathroom who'd said something to her. Maybe one of those people from

Cox who blamed her for not making it to the state finals last year.

Man, I'd like two minutes alone with the jerks from her old school. I had a sudden urge to wrap Ali up in my arms and protect her from all the small-minded and insensitive comments. Only, she didn't need me to do that. She'd been strong enough to handle all that ugliness on her own. I respected the heck out of her. I was sinking fast and hard for Ali Frost. And I was okay with that.

23

BUTT UGLY OR COMPLETE COWARDS

Ali

Llama farts! I couldn't believe I was doing this. My hands shook as I fished around in Dax's athletic bag for his playbook. I didn't want to do this but we hadn't figured out another option to save the rabbits. Justin Bieber's butt! I was pissed at those goons for dragging me into this mess. If I ever figured out who they were, I would make them sorry they messed with me and my friends.

Scooting further into the truck, I shoved my hand deeper into the bag, frantically feeling my way around. Shoulder pads… chest pad…T-shirt (I hoped)…cleats…um, not sure…smooth, plastic, triangle shape—ack! Letting go quickly, I moved on, my fingers running along what felt like a spiral of flexible plastic. Please yes! I slid my fingers over checking and—success!— pages. Got it! I wasted no time pulling it out and shoving it deep down into my bowling bag. I zipped both bags closed and slithered back out of the truck.

Scratching a big fat line through cat burglar on my list of possible career choices, I locked up Dax's truck and leaned my forehead against the cool glass of the passenger window, waiting for my heart rate to slow down. Because oh my word, I was—

"Everything okay?" Dax. His deep voice sounded right behind me, shocking my heart, so no paddles necessary.

Holy cats, he'd scared me. I turned toward him, leaning against his truck since nerves had my knees too shaky and weak to do their job.

"I...I'm fine. It took me longer to find my...my, um..." My what? Tampon? Absolutely not. Lip gloss? He knew I didn't wear any. "Pain medication. I've got a headache trying to evolve into a migraine like someone handed Wild Pikachu a thunder stone."

"You should have said something." He pulled me into his chest and rubbed his big hand on my back. "Should I take you home?"

I exhaled the breath I'd been holding for the last ten minutes —a new record for humankind. Or maybe a guilty conscience suspended time and it just felt that long.

"That would probably be best," I said, loading a second scoop of guilt on my guilt sundae. Stealing and lying. "I'm sorry about ruining your Friday night."

"*Our* Friday night." He opened the door and helped me into the seat. "You didn't ruin it. I'm fine with an early night since I've got to get up early tomorrow. Coach called an early morning practice to watch some film for Friday's game."

Dax dropped me off and I proceeded to spend the next two hours driving myself crazy waiting until it was time to leave.

I shut my eyes and imagined a world where high school football was a simple game kids played just for fun. One where football wasn't the staple meal everyone dug into like a Thanksgiving feast. Where it wasn't more important than water in a desert. One where you could slice open a vein and not bleed high school football.

But when I opened my eyes, I was still in Texas.

* * *

Tonight was my turn to drive the getaway car. Gaby's host family had taken her to a rodeo in Del Rio, but all the other girls were gathered at Rowena's for a "slumber party." After everyone was in, I gripped the steering wheel with my sweaty palms and drove to the old drive in.

"I hate this," I said. "I hate having to sneak around. I hate lying to Dax. When I think about handing the playbook to those two goons my chest vibrates like a volcano ready to erupt."

"I'm right there with you," Bhakti said, reaching out from the back seat to give my shoulder a squeeze. "Let's get it over with, rescue the bunnies, and hope somehow they get caught."

"If we can't figure out who it is, at the very least I want Karma to knock them on their butts," Mari said.

I stopped the car at the entrance. No one even bothered locking the place up anymore because teenagers always found a way in anyway.

"I just want to say…thanks. Thanks for not letting me do this on my own."

"Giiirrrl, that's sweet—but stop delaying." Shani sent me a knowing look.

Right. I was. The longer I stalled only dragged this whole ordeal out. I pressed on the gas and drove Milo in. The electricity had been shut off when it closed and the ginormous movie screen was tattered and torn. The lot, a dirt field with scattered patches of grass and weeds, looked like a graveyard and the steel speaker posts stood like row upon row of skeletons.

I parked in spot P-7 as directed. After shutting off the car and the headlights, I reached under my seat and pulled out the playbook. Minutes ticked off like hours while we waited.

"Maybe they chickened out," Rowena said.

"If it weren't for the rabbits, that would be awesome," Mari said.

It was a lose-lose situation. Either we wouldn't rescue the mascots or I'd carry the weight of guilt over stealing Dax's playbook. Aaaand I was possibly helping another team beat our own team. Yay! Another school about to adopt the Ali Frost must die theme. That should be super fun.

"Hey! I just thought of something!" Bhakti leaned up from the back seat. "We can eliminate all the teams that don't make the playoffs."

"That still leaves about ten schools and fifty players per team," I said. "Five hundred potential suspects."

"Yikes. Never mind."

The sound of tires crunching on gravel had us all sitting up and taking a collective breath before we got out of the car to wait. They parked their car next to the boarded up concession stand—too far away to read their license plate—and exited the car along with the rabbit cage. The slam of their doors reverberated down my spine.

"Meet us at C-11!" one of them called.

"C-11? What the heck?" Shani grumbled. "Now they're yanking our chain."

"They're keeping us from getting a good look at their tags," Bhakti said.

Together we walked up seven rows and over four spaces.

"Anyone else feel like Ron and Harry in the game of wizard chess?"

The goons walked across and then down until we stood facing each other. They wore masks. Figures. Freddy Krueger and an Orc.

"Y'all are either butt ugly or complete cowards," Shani said.

"Or both," I said. "Ugly and gutless."

"Shut it." Krueger lifted the blanket on the cage, shining a flashlight on it. "Now let's see the playbook."

My gut clenched over what I was about to do. I glanced over at the girls, shaking my head. "This is so wrong."

Mari grabbed my forearm. "We need to get the rabbits."

"You're right. It's just—" I didn't want to do this.

The Orc growled, shining his flashlight at the book in my hands. "We're not falling for a fake one again. Read me the rattlesnake play so we know it's real."

Oh, it was real. All too real. But I fanned through the book until I found it. "QB fakes a handoff to RB, side-laterals to the TE and—"

"Not a fake. Now give us the rabbits," Mari demanded in a voice so angry even I jumped.

"Playbook," Kruger held his beefy hand out for it.

I extended my arm out, the playbook shaking like crazy in my trembling hand. Kruger wrapped his sausage-link fingers around it and pulled but I couldn't let go. I couldn't.

"What was that?" Rowena whipped her head to the right over by the ticket office. "Did you guys hear something?"

"Nothing!" The Orc said. "You're hearing things."

"Or trying to delay so you can trick us again." Kruger pulled harder on the playbook. "Let go!"

"No! I can't! I can't do it!" I grabbed the playbook with both hands and pulled with everything I had. "I'm not giving it to you!"

Kruger pulled harder and it slipped from my hands like a soup sandwich.

"I've got the rabbits!" Mari yelled.

"Let's go." Kruger jerked his head at Orc-face and turned, acting like he'd done no more than check out a book from the library.

"Noooo! Give it back!" I jumped on his back, wrapped my arms around his thick neck, all while flailing my hand around trying to grab the playbook.

Shani and Bhakti piled on too, trying to stop him. But he

shook us off like a wet dog sheds water. The three of us landed hard, strewn about on the ground. By the time I got my breath back and struggled to sit up, all I could do was watch the goons toss the playbook in the trunk and pull out of the parking lot, their taillights disappearing quickly.

I fell back with a groan and lay in the parking lot, run over by guilt.

"Hey, we got Mr. and Ms. Jackalope back," Mari said trying to be all silver-lining.

"I've got to tell Dax," I said. Only I really, really didn't want to tell Dax.

"This wasn't your fault," Shani said.

"I still have to tell him."

I stared up at the night sky. Only a few stars glimmered down on me. Too many clouds. So, so different from the sky when I stargazed with Dax. Like without Dax my world was a darker place.

24

HEY, UNIVERSE, IF YOU'RE
LISTENING...

Ali

ON A GUILT TRIP, SATURDAY/SUNDAY

I hated myself. I was a big fat chicken. There had been plenty of
time over the weekend when I could have told Dax about the
playbook. *Should* have told Dax. Guilt collapsed that starry
feeling I'd been floating on the last few weeks, leaving a giant
sucking black hole in my chest.

But I was afraid of losing what we had. Losing him.

I'd lost so many people in my life over the last year and a
half. It seemed unfair I had to lose Dax too. Amazingly, once
again, over something someone else had done. Mostly.

Ugh. Yes, I had handed over the playbook, but I'd tried to get
it back. Where the heck was the kid who'd set this whole thing
up? Who'd agreed to hand over the playbook? Why did the
universe think it was fair to put me in the wrong place at the
wrong time and suck me into another mess? Heck, I hadn't even
recovered from the last one.

I spent the weekend running worst-case-scenarios through
my head. What if I told Dax? Just told him flat out what

happened. He cared about me. At least he said he liked me. Would he listen calmly and see my side of the situation? Or would he blame me and walk away?

Then of course there was that stupid expression about letting something you love go and if it was truly meant to be it will come back to you. Sounded easy, right? It wasn't.

First, because how do I let Dax go when all I wanted to do was throw my arms around him and never let him go?

Second was the "it will come back to you" part. It's possible that when he came back—if he came back—he'd be as angry as a longhorn steer on branding day. Anger aimed directly at me. Was it wrong of me to want to avoid that?

Yes. Because nothing counted if I wasn't honest.

Which was why on Saturday morning I tried to girl-up and tell him. I took the easy way out and tried to do it over a text.

Me: You there?

Dax: For you, always.

Me: There's something I need to tell you...

Dax: ?

Me: ...

Dax: You know you can tell me anything, right?

Me: Yeah, it's just—

Me:

Me:

Dax: Hey, you can trust me.

Me:

Dax: Ali?

Me: ...

Dax: It's okay. You know where to find me. ;) Tell me when you're ready.

Me: I... Yeah. Okay.

Dax: Want to do something tonight?

Me: I can't. Plans with friends.

Dax: Sunday?

Me: Oh...I've got a calc test I need to study for.
Dax: The downfall of dating a brainy girl.
Me:
Dax: You totally know I'm kidding, right?
Me: Oh, yeah. Ha ha. See you Monday.

See? I tried to do the right thing and tell him. FAIL. Yes, being busy the rest of the weekend was me avoiding having to face Dax. And my guilt. But I actually did have plans on Saturday night. My friends and I went dress shopping. Mari was attending the dance with Nathan Baker and the others were going stag. So if you've ever wondered about that eternal question, how many nerds does it take to shop for a dress? The answer is six.

The calc test was real too, although I probably overdid the studying. Nothing like avoiding facing something to make a person super conscientious. I picked up my phone and hit the video record.

"How did I get here? Everything is a tangled mess and each move I make only tightens the knots." I blew out a breath and pushed my bangs out of my eyes. "Well, mission accomplished. I gave Dax's playbook to a rival team. I didn't want to. Not at all. But I didn't know any other way to get the mascots back. I feel horrible, but I'd have felt worse if the bunnies had died. And Mari. Oh gosh, that might have broken Mari.

"How did a case of mistaken identity get this messed up? I'd love five minutes alone with the person who started this whole cascade of awful. Who at Jackson would sell out the football team like that?"

I stared silently into my phone while I thought about the football team and Dax. The more I thought about it, the easier I could breathe. I relaxed my white-knuckled grip and let the worry float away. Dax may not trust his own talent, but I did.

Dad had nothing but praise for Dax's ability. He'd said Dax was the full package: athletic, smart, great instincts, and a natural leader.

"Here's the plan," I said into my phone. "I'll try to tell Dax one more time. But if I lose my nerve again, it might not be that big of a deal. So we don't know what team the goons play for, but Jackson's football team is strong this year. Dax is one of the best quarterbacks in the state. Good enough that the playbook probably won't make a bit of difference."

Pressing the circle at the bottom of my screen, I stopped recording. I hadn't had much good luck the last year and a half. In fact, things had pretty much sucked. So it only seemed fair that something should finally go my way. I was due, darn it.

I stabbed the record button with my thumb and looked into my screen.

"Hey, universe, if you're listening... How about the good guys win this time and the bad guys lose? And...could I— pretty, pretty please—end up with Dax DeLeon? Because I really like him. Seriously like. There's something special about him. About...us. So, I'm just a girl, standing in front of the universe, asking you to not mess this up."

A WIN-WIN FOR US BOTH

Dax

Spirit Week, Monday Morning, "B" Day

Happy Monday morning, Jackalopes! Our good news of the day: Mr. and Ms. Jackalope are back!

Cool. Senior pranks were a rite of passage and sometimes impressive. Like two years ago when the guys from shop class put the car on the roof. Or last year when two girls on the physics club filled Principal Barstow's office with Styrofoam peanuts. Stealing the bunnies though, not cool. It was pretty amazing that no one seemed to know who'd taken them. Normally gossip spread like a brushfire on a windy summer day around school. Like the gossip about the cops busting up Walker's party Friday night. My phone lit up with texts within minutes of the sirens.

Sitting in first period listening to the fall out—who got drinking tickets, who got suspended, and who got grounded for life—had me thanking my lucky stars Ali's headache probably saved us from being thick in the middle of that mess.

It's spirit week! Pull out those crazy socks for tomorrow!

Spirit week. I enjoyed the build up toward Friday night's game, but the dress up days were not geared to guys. Take crazy sock day for example... Crazy sock day for a guy meant not wearing the same pair of socks two days in a row.

Wacky hair Wednesday.

Nope. Excluding Slick Baker who always had his head shaved in a mohawk for his punk band and maybe the handful of guys who'd dye their hair, just no.

Charity Thursday. Bring those cans!

Okay, guys could do that. We could donate cans for the food pantry or a dollar to fight cancer. But charity Thursday used to be pajama Thursday. Until two years ago when some guys from the lacrosse team came to school in their "pajamas" aka boxers —and only boxers.

Don't forget Friday is blue-out day or wear your sports team jersey. Show your school spirit for the pep rally!

There you go. This was the day guys embraced. It was easy and you didn't feel like a dweeb. Blue T-shirt or a favorite team jersey. Pro or high school; didn't matter. Boom. Done.

Let's fill the stands this Friday night to cheer on our varsity football team as they take on the Travis Titans. Help them wrap up the season strong!

"Dude, we're already in the playoffs!" Jake slapped me on the back.

"Don't get cocky," I said. "You know what Coach says: You get cocky; you get careless. I'm taking it one game at a time."

After the game, dance the night away at the winter dance. There will be a table outside of the cafeteria all week selling tickets. This year's theme is "Wish Upon a Star."

Wish upon a star? I grinned as I thought of Ali and our first date under the stars. I pulled out my phone and stealth-texted her when Mrs. March's back was turned.

Me: See you at lunch?

Ali: Sorry. Promised my friends I'd eat with them this week.

Me: *Gotcha. Pep rally on Friday?*

Ali: *Can't. Allergic.*

Me: *Haha. But seriously.*

Ali: *Serious. That much school spirit gives me hives.*

Me: *At least I'll see you in bowling class. I'm pumped for our game Friday, but I'm also looking forward to the dance with you after.*

Ali: *Dax...I need to tell you...that...*

I waited watching those three bouncing dots appear and disappear once, twice and a third time before disappearing. Was she trying to back out of the dance with me? Had she changed her mind? No lie, my chest felt like when I hit the ground hard after getting sacked.

Me: *??*

Ali: *I'm...wearing pants to the dance. Dresses aren't my thing.*

I puffed out the breath that had been stuck trapped in my lungs.

Me: *You could wear a clown suit and I wouldn't care.*

Ali: *A clown suit, huh?*

Me: *Okay, maybe not a clown suit, but your bowling shirt or your cut-off sweats. What I'm saying is I just like being with you.*

No response from Ali. Crap. I shouldn't have added that last part. Yeah, too much. I probably freaked her out. I was figuring out what to text that might water it down when she responded.

Ali: *Me too. A lot.*

Boom went my heart. It felt like someone shot me with a paintball gun only instead of paint it was warm, gooey caramel.

Friday afternoon's pep rally was fun. It was pretty much the same as it was before each game. The cheerleaders cheered. The marching band played. The drum line got everyone lit up. So by the time our football team ran out onto the gym floor the whole student body went wild. Applause, whistles, hoots and hollers.

The school spirit would carry us onto the field pumped up and ready to win.

Ali had texted me good luck and I liked knowing she would be in the stands to watch. Plus along with her bowling teammates she'd said her dad was attending. Coach Frost in the bleachers watching was both exciting and nerve-wracking. Which was why I didn't mention that to the rest of the team. I wasn't kidding when I'd said he was a legend in the football world. No point in adding more stress to the team.

The team suited up in the locker room, everyone going through their usual pre-game routines. Pump-up music from Garcia's phone, a little smack talk about how we were going to chew up the other team, and then we circled in for Coach.

"Don't think about next week. Or the next game. It's only tonight. Only this game." Coach Devlin ran his steely gaze over all our faces. "Stay focused, play clean, and give your best effort on every single play. It's as simple as that."

There was nothing like running onto the field on a Friday night in Texas. Nothing. The air was electric, the fans rabid for the team, and the marching band pulling everyone together and building up the crescendo of excitement.

That excitement stayed high as Travis matched us score for score throughout the whole game. Yes, I had one bad throw that led to a Travis interception and touch down. I also had two stellar passes that scored for us. The game was tied with less than two minutes to go when our TE Jacoby fumbled the ball on a hard tackle. Travis recovered the ball and ran it down to their nineteen. It was an ugly final two minutes. Standing helplessly on the sidelines watching them score in the last thirty seconds was the worst. The final whistle barely penetrated my brain.

"You were great out there, Dax." Kev smiled and raised his hand in the air for a high five.

"Thanks, Kev." I slapped my hand against his. Needless to say it lacked Kev's enthusiasm. "But we lost."

"Only by a field goal. It was close, and we're still going to the playoffs." Kev gave me a pat on my shoulder pads. "Plus, you'll be crowned Mr. Jackalope at the dance tonight. You get to wear the crown and the sash. It's exciting."

"Hey, it might be one of the other guys," I said.

"I voted for you." He smiled and adjusted his ball cap. "You deserve it."

Deserved it? For what? Not for my play as quarterback. Not lately.

"Thanks." It was almost impossible to stay down around Kev. If his grin didn't get you, then his positive attitude would. But even Kev's positivity wasn't helping.

I didn't like eating a loss. Not a single serving of it. Not when our team was out-matched or out-played. Not when a ref's bad call went against us. Not when one of my teammates made a costly mistake. But the worst loss to choke down was when it was my fault. Like tonight.

When I arrived at the hotel where the dance was being held, I texted Ali. We'd agreed she'd catch a ride with one of her friends and I'd meet her here after running home to shower and change. By the time I opened the doors to the hotel ballroom, I still hadn't locked down my disappointment. Until I saw Ali.

Wow. My girl was gorgeous. She stood waiting for me near the door, a tentative smile on her face.

"Sorry about the game," she said.

"You know what? I'm not letting the loss ruin our night. So we don't have a perfect record. Like Kev reminded me, we're still heading to the playoffs, right?"

"R-right." She bit her lip and nodded.

"Besides… Look at you. You're beautiful. When you said you were wearing pants—I didn't imagine this." Her silky pants and matching top were the same midnight blue of the sky we'd lain under. They were soft and flowing and totally her. Unique in a sea of sparkly, strapless gowns. Her red hair was loose and curling over her shoulders and down her back. "Very hot."

"I'm not hot." She blushed and gave me a soft punch in my biceps.

"Sorry. Overruled." I took her hand and led her out to the crowded dance floor, pulling her into my arms. "Come on, gummy bear, let's dance."

Ali laughed up at me before settling against me, wrapping her arms around my neck. "Okay, Kevin Bacon."

"Hey! You joke, but wait until you see my dance moves. I guarantee you'll be impressed."

"Guarantee, huh?"

"Yes. If you're not impressed, I'll give you a kiss. But if you are impressed, you can kiss me."

She shook her head with a smile. "So, I kiss you either way? Something sounds wrong about that."

"It's a win-win for us both." I winked since by now the wink was an old joke between us. Sure enough, she snickered. "And if that's wrong, I don't ever want to be right."

26

YOU KNOW ME

Ali

We danced. We laughed. We had the best time. The most fun moment? Seeing Dax's football players mixing it up on the dance floor with the bowling nerds.

To say that event blasted shockwaves through the popular clique would be an understatement. Some of them (aka Paige and her gang) stood staring from the edge of the dance floor. If their eyes had been laser-guided missiles, everyone on the bowling team would be history. For the few minutes that they weren't at the top of the social pecking order they were lost. They had no idea how to just "be."

I spent half a second thinking about them before jumping onto the end of the dance train weaving its way around the room to "Love Train."

"I need some water," I said, happily out of breath from dancing non-stop since Dax had arrived. I blotted my damp overheated face with a napkin. "And a chance to catch my breath."

Dax wrapped his arm around my shoulders and steered us

through the crowd over to the refreshment tables. In the time it took me to drink half a water bottle, Dax downed two.

We nibbled on pretzels, mini cupcakes, and M&M's before Dax pulled us back to the dance floor.

"Dax, seriously, I need to rest."

"I know," he said. "Which is why I requested a slow song."

"Oh, nice." I stepped into the circle of his arms and rested my head on his shoulder as some country singer sang, "Baby, I'm Crazy 'Bout You." I wanted to capture this perfect moment in a bottle. The feel of Dax's strong arms around me and the press of his lips to my temple. My heart floated like a shimmering bubble rising on a whisper of a breeze. Every color of the refracted rainbow shining brightly. It had been so long since I'd had this feeling. So long that I'd forgotten what it felt like—but I was happy.

I tilted my head back to look at Dax. He must have sensed it because he opened his dark fathomless eyes and the air between us sparked and sizzled.

"Thank you," I said.

He didn't ask for what. He simply smiled at me. Not his cocky grin, or his wide flirty one. It was small and real and went all the way to his eyes. I lifted up onto my toes and pressed my lips to his.

It was the best kiss ever. A hot, firm, breath-stealing, heart-pounding kiss. The top of my head tingled like I was blasting through the atmosphere. It was all rockets and fireworks and—

"Break it up, Ms. Frost."

Coach Diamond?

"Eeep!" I pulled my lips from Dax's, heat flushing into my cheeks.

"Sorry about that," Dax said.

"Hey, I kissed you. I'm not sorry."

The microphone sounded that high-pitched screech, getting everyone's attention to the front stage. Mrs. March, the hardest

English teacher in the school and the faculty mentor for our senior class, stood waiting for it to get quiet.

"Good evening, Jackalopes! It's time to announce this year's Mr. and Ms. Jackalope. Without further ado, please welcome Paige Smith, the head of the Winter Dance planning committee."

There were claps and whistles from around the room. Some woo girls woo'ed.

"Hello, party people! I hold the envelope with the names of the winners in my hand!" Paige raised the envelope over her head as kids screamed. "But first… It's tradition that each nominee makes a short video. So here they are in their own words—and of course, mine—the winter court nominees!"

A large screen lowered behind Paige and one of the techie computer kids worked the equipment to start the videos. First, and probably the most popular, were the videos for Mr. Jackalope.

Dax flashed up on the screen, standing on the football field in his practice jersey looking hot and sweaty like he'd just finished practice. He smiled into the camera and said, "Hey guys. I'm supposed to tell you why I deserve to be crowned Mr. Jackalope over the other nominees. To be honest, I can't do that. I can think of a lot of guys equally, if not more, deserving. But I do consider the nomination an honor. Thanks." He threw in a wink that had the girls sighing and cheering for him.

Up next was Grady, standing in his garage holding his precious Fender guitar. (Yes, the one I almost ran over.) "Grady here. You know, I know DeLeon, and I'll bet he's going to pretend to be all modest and say he doesn't deserve Mr. Jackalope. First of all, don't fall for his modest act. Second, I hope you all voted for me. I may not be a top student and I may have skipped a class or two—kidding, Mrs. Baxter. I'd never skip your class—but, let's just say DeLeon wouldn't look as good on the field if I wasn't so good at catching his lame passes. Plus, I play a righteous guitar. Rock on, my people."

The last video was from Zaevion, the senior class vice president and captain of the debate team. Nerdy, cute, and concise. "I'm not a hot jock like DeLeon or a cool rocker like Grady. But one day I might perform life-saving surgery on you, so be smart and vote for me."

While everyone cheered for all three guys, I nervously ran what I'd said on my video through my head for the thousandth time. I remember filming it last week with Rowena's help. I'd meant to keep mine short and sweet but then something else had erupted from deep down.

Hi. I'm Ali Frost. I'm honored for the nomination, although I know so many girls at Jackson more deserving than I am. But if I were to win—I'll accept it for all the bowlers, the nerds, the geeks, the wall-flowers, the rejects, and the outcast. The ones who aren't afraid to be different.

See why I was nervous? I know. I'd gone full *Breakfast Club.* You should never go full *Breakfast Club.* But it was too late to change it now.

"Here we go! Equal time for the ladies," Paige said into the mic as the next set of videos started.

First up was Paige. She managed to wear three different outfits in her one minute video. Of course she looked stunning in each. She didn't actually say anything but did a quick cheer for herself which ended in the splits. Lots of kids cheered for her.

Next up was Lacey Trueheart. Lacey was the captain of the pep club. She was smart, popular, and nice. She waved and smiled into the camera. "Hi, gang. Thanks for the nomination. My goal every day is to spread school spirit and kindness around like confetti. You can never have too much of either, right? No matter who gets crowned Ms. Jackalope, all I have to say is… Go Jackson!!" Huge applause for Lacey followed.

Then it was my turn. My stomach twisted and my mind readied. *Hi. I'm Ali Frost. I would...*

Only that wasn't what I said. Not. At. All. No. The Ali up on the huge screen pointed directly at the camera and said...

"It doesn't matter what other kids think. I like myself and that's enough. You've got this, Ali Frost."

What? No. This wasn't my video. I mean, it was, but not the one I'd turned in.

My stomach twisted and my mind scrambled to grasp what I was seeing—heck, what I was saying—as kids laughed and giggled at my video.

"Who does Dax DeLeon think he is? He's too cocky by far."

Oh no, oh no, oh no.

The laughter grew around the room like a wave about to break as apparently everyone thought this was a joke. Even Dax laughed and gave my hand a squeeze thinking it was funny. This was so not funny. This was wrong. These were clips from my private video diary. There was no way I'd turned in the wrong video. These clips were cut and spliced together.

"If I had a way to knock that cheeky, arrogant, swaggering smirk off his face, I'd do it."

The mood turned in the ballroom. My confusion morphed into shock. My heart raced like I was standing at the edge of a cliff with the earth crumbling beneath my feet. The light-hearted laughter shifted around me. To uncertainty. To disquiet. Whispers and mumbles rippled through the room.

"Mission accomplished. I gave Dax's playbook to a rival team."

The last video clip faded into a photograph. A zoomed-in photo of me handing the playbook over to the goon. Only the goon didn't make the photo other than his hand. It was just me. And my voice repeating over and over...

"If I had a way to knock that cheeky, arrogant, swaggering smirk off his face, I'd do it."

Pandemonium broke out and Dax's hand jerked away from

mine. The atmospheric pressure rose as the whole place sucked in a collective gasp. Angry faces whipped toward me. But I didn't care about any of those faces. There was only one face I cared about.

I looked up at Dax and saw him process everything as if in slow motion. Confusion slid into pain and pain hardened into anger until his eyes blazed down on me.

"It's not what it looks like, Dax. It's not."

His eyes chilled to an arctic frost and he took a step back from me.

"You can't believe that," I said, my voice shaking. "You know me."

"I don't think I do," he said.

"You do. You know me. Only you have to trust yourself to see it." I paused, waiting, but all he did was shake his head and take another step back. And another.

Anger pushed in at me from every direction. My worst nightmare. But I'd been here before. I'd been crushed under the weight of it once. I refused to do it again. I clenched my jaw, lifted my chin high, turned, and walked out of the dance.

Did I think Dax would run after me and give me a chance to explain? No. I didn't. Because one year ago I'd learned how hive-minded people were. Even the people you thought you could count on. It took courage and strength to break from the pack.

I guess even the great Dax DeLeon wasn't strong enough for that.

2 7

BLINDSIDED

Dax

Crash & Burn @ the Winter Dance, 10:38 p.m.

What the hell just happened? Ali had stolen my play book and handed it over to a rival team? I couldn't believe it. I didn't want to believe it.

Except she'd been caught. She couldn't lie because the photograph revealed the ugly truth. Yet she tried to. *It's not what it looks like, Dax.* Talk about being blindsided.

Shit, it hurt. Like a punch to the face.

A hand on my shoulder cut through my pain.

"Dude, I'm sorry," TJ said.

"I think I'm the one that should be apologizing. To you and the team." I still couldn't wrap my head around it.

There was an angry buzz of chatter throughout the place. A flurry of movement up on the stage, and then Mrs. March took control.

"So, that was interesting," she said. "Of course, Principal Barstow and Coach Devlin will be looking in to this situation. Let's move on and announce the winners. This year's Mr. and

Ms. Jackalope are"—Mrs. March tore open the envelope and shook open the folded sheet of paper—"Paige Smith and Dax DeLeon! Come on up for your coronation!"

Paige smiled like she'd won a million-dollar lottery, happily returning to the stage while her friends cheered.

The last thing I wanted to do was walk up on that stage, but TJ's hand on my shoulder pushed me forward.

"Just get it over with," TJ said.

With a nod, I pulled myself together and made my way up next to Paige.

"I had a premonition we'd both win." She wrapped her hands around my arm and smiled up at me. There was an edge to her smile that I couldn't quite interpret. Confident? Possessive? Smug? "And here we are. Together again."

Together again? The girl was delusional. I stood there, my jaw clenched, muscles tense, and my stomach heavy like I'd swallowed a boulder while Gwen slid the sash over Paige's head and across her shoulder. Lacey Trueheart helped with the crown. Paige waved like an actual royal princess.

Next it was my turn. Lacey and Gwen came over with the sash and crown. Instead of letting them place them on me though, I held out my hands for them. Looking at the sash in one hand and the crown in my other, I nodded and stepped up to the microphone.

"To me, being crowned Mr. Jackalope represents being a positive force at Jackson. I know a guy who's a veritable tornado of positivity. His pride and love of our school could fill this room and it still wouldn't all fit. He inspires and lifts up everyone in his path. He cheers on every sport—even the debate and chess teams. I dare anyone to talk with him and not walk away with a smile. He's selfless, dedicating his time as the student manager of our football and lacrosse teams. If all that isn't enough, he also pulled off a miracle. Because of him, we actually look forward to eating in the cafeteria...on Wednesdays."

"My stomach thanks you!" someone in the back yelled.

Laughter blossomed along with some loud whistles.

"This crown belongs to Kevin Grace," I said.

The room exploded in cheers. The football and lacrosse players chanted his name. *Kev. Kev. Kev. Kev.*

"Get on up here, Kev."

Kev jogged up and onto the stage, accompanied by ear-shattering applause the whole way. Lacey helped me put the sash and crown on him, which was challenging because he kept pumping both fists in the air to celebrate.

I left the stage as someone from the yearbook staff took pictures of this year's Mr. and Ms. Jackalope. When I left, I didn't wait around. I kept right on walking, past my teammates and straight out of the ballroom. Once in the wide hallway, I escaped out the closest door and found myself next to the outdoor pool.

My phone was blowing up, so I turned it off, and shoved it back into my pocket. I needed to talk to TJ and then the rest of the team. But right now I needed a few minutes to myself. My head felt like a giant bell that had been clanged with Thor's hammer and the reverberations were still pulsing through my brain.

Feelings fought each other in my chest until they were a tangled incoherent mess. They wrestled and every few minutes a new one rose to the top. Shock. Pain. Anger. Confusion.

I threw myself onto one of the lounge chairs and stared up at the sky. The light scattering of stars overhead were a painful reminder—a pale mockery—of what I'd had with Ali.

What I couldn't avoid was the fact that Ali did dislike me at first. Strongly disliked. But I would have sworn that changed. Grown into something altogether different. Two people caring about each other. Slowly and tentatively spreading roots deeper.

Stronger. Dazzling in the starlight. Being with Ali had felt like fresh air and sunshine. Honest. Real.

That's what got me—everything with Ali had felt real. The joke was on me because based on her video and that photo it had all been a lie. Dammit. It hadn't felt like a lie. And just like that, anger horse-collared all my other emotions, clawing its way up my chest like a hulking monster.

"Hey, Dax." It was Paige, standing a few feet away. She moved closer until she stood right next to my chair. "Are you okay?"

"Yep. Absolutely fine." I moved quickly, swinging my legs around until I was sitting on the side of the lounger, legs splayed in a "V" and feet on the ground ready to make a quick exit. Paige was the last person I wanted to talk with right now. Okay, maybe the second to last.

"I'm so sorry about what happened." She sat next to me, so close our arms rubbed together. "It wasn't your fault. She fooled everyone, but a person can't hide who they are."

"No, I guess not," I said.

"It always comes out in the end." Paige slid her hand onto my thigh, moving closer until our faces were only a foot apart. "You've got to be careful who you trust."

Needing space, I leaned forward away from her touch, rested my elbows on my knees, and stared down at my hands clasped in front of me.

"You think you know someone and then they show you who they really are."

You know me. You do. You know me.

"That girl has some nerve. To think you lost the game because of her. I know how much you hate to lose. You have every right to be angry. The whole team is pissed about it."

No kidding. My stomach clenched thinking about the conversation still to come with my teammates.

"I guess the rumors about her were true," Paige said with a shake of her head.

"What rumors?"

"That everyone at Cox hated her. She must get off on attention. Why else risk becoming the most hated girl at Jackson too?"

"Not to be rude, but I don't want to talk about it." I turned my head to glance at Paige, hoping she'd take the hint and leave. "I don't even want to think about it right now."

"I understand. But if you ever need someone to listen, or you know, whatever, I'm here for you." She rubbed her hand on my shoulder and then slid it down to squeeze my biceps. She leaned in close, so close I could feel her breath on my face. "I'm always here for you, Dax."

Whoa, no. If someone yelled snake, I couldn't have stood any faster. I mean, I flew out of the chair and put lots of air between us. I knew what she was offering. You know what she was offering, right? You might find this hard to believe, being that I'm a jock and all, but I didn't even have to think about her offer.

Not for a second.

Sure, I was an angry mess right now, but doing "whatever" with Paige was the last thing I needed. Or wanted. Ali had run a stake through my heart. It was going to take time for my heart to heal. Especially because right now, I wasn't sure she hadn't delivered a fatal blow.

THAT'S NOT HOW THIS WORKS

Ali

11:05 P.M.

I'd taken an Uber home since Dax was supposed to be my ride. Maybe I'm some sort of masochist because I spent the duration of the ride scrolling through all the lovely comments and suggestions about what I should do to myself, where I should go, and basically what an all-around horrific person I was on my Facebook page. There was something about all that ugliness that took my mind off of Dax.

I'd hoped to slide quietly in the door and disappear in my room, but Dad was sitting at the kitchen island eating one of his three-inch-high sandwich concoctions.

"Hey, Ali-Cat. I thought I wouldn't see you until after midnight."

"Well, here I am. Ta-da."

"How was it? Did you have a fun time?"

"The dancing was fun." That was true.

"And?" He had his proud papa grin on his face. "Are you going to tell me who won Mr. and Ms. Jackalope?"

"Oh, I have no idea. I left before it was announced."

"Why would you do that? Both you and Dax were nominated."

"About that…Dax and I are over."

"Over?"

"Yep." My lips didn't even wobble and my voice was steady.

"Do you want to talk about it?"

"Nope. Not really."

"Al—"

"Honest, Dad. I'm good." I faked a yawn and walked down the hallway to my room.

If you thought I was escaping to my room to cry—you'd be wrong. No tears. No anger. No anything. I was downright stoic. As I changed into sweats and a T-shirt, I mentally prepped for the solo expedition I'd be making through the rest of senior year. Brick by brick, I'd rebuild the wall around my heart. The one I'd torn down to let Dax in.

I fell face first onto my bed, like a falling tree after a chain saw slices through its trunk.

This was nothing new. I'd been here before.

So Dax hated me.

So the football team hated me.

So the whole school hated me.

Whatever.

I only had to get through—how many more days? I had no idea. When had I stopped counting? I did some quick math… one-hundred five more days.

"Ali?" Dad knocked on my door. "Someone's here to see you."

Dax? My heart lurched and I flipped onto my back, blinking up at the ceiling while something light and frothy bubbled up in my chest. Until I recalled his cold, hard eyes staring into mine. No. It wasn't Dax. "I'm not really up for—"

"Giiirrrl, I'm not leaving." Shani sounded like she had her face pressed against the other side of my door. "So either let me in or I'll hang out and watch the *Say Yes to the Dress* marathon with your dad."

"Ali, honey, if you have any love in your heart for me, you'll open the door."

I opened it to save my dad and let Shani in, only all the girls spilled in behind her.

"How are you doing?" Mari ran her worried gaze over my face.

"I'm fine."

"She's not fine," Bhakti said.

"Why wouldn't I be fine?" I grabbed Mr. Pinky, the stuffed rabbit I'd had since fourth grade, hugging him into my chest. "I lost a guy I should never have been with in the first place. The entire school hates me for selling out our football team. Due to the photographic evidence, there is a one-hundred percent chance I'll be having a heart-to-heart talk with Principal Barstow on Monday."

"I doubt everyone hates you," Gaby said.

I picked up my phone, brought up my Facebook page, and handed it to Gaby. They all moved in to look.

"Oh boy." Rowena frowned.

"Oh my. Okay, so you're right. Everyone hates you," Bhakti said.

"Who cares if everyone hates her?" Shani asked.

I shrugged. "Well, it's not fun..."

"What I mean is we've got bigger things to discuss," Shani said.

"Um...bigger than Dax DeLeon turning out to be a jerk and"—Mari grabbed my phone from Gaby—"two-hundred thirty seven hate filled comments on her Facebook page?"

My stomach churned at the number. Déjà vomit.

"Yes!" Shani said. "Who swapped out Ali's video and how did they make that fake one?"

I cleared my throat. "Those were clips from my video diary.

Random clips spliced together to make it sound, well, not random."

"Isn't that on your private YouTube channel?" Rowena asked.

"Yeah. And you guys are the only ones I told." My gaze ran around the room, looking at each face, wondering if one of them was involved. My gut said no, but my head...

"Whoa, Ali. You can't think one of us told anyone about your video diary." Gaby frowned at me. "We'd never do that."

"You know what? It doesn't matter. It's okay," I said. "It's done. I've been through this before. I'll be fine. You all should go home."

"What are you talking about?" Shani asked.

"I was the only one in the photo. You guys are out of it."

"That's not how this works," Bhakti said. "We're your friends. Good times. Bad times. You're stuck with us."

"Ugh." I threw my hands in the air which accidently sent Mr. Pinky sailing across the room. "I don't want you all to become targets because of me."

"Sorry, but it's not up to you." Gaby plopped onto my bed, making herself comfortable like she wasn't leaving any time soon.

"But—"

"Nope." Mari shook her head. "We're all in this together. But here's the thing—you're going to have to trust us."

I still felt beat up from the last time the people I thought I could trust had abandoned me. My friends. My own mother. Trust never worked out well for me. Except for my dad, not ever really.

"Hey, don't look like that. You never talked about it, but we heard the rumors about what happened at Cox. We're not like your old friends."

"That's right! We don't abandon our friends. That's a promise."

Not once during this whole evening had I broken. Not one single tear.

Until now. Cue the waterworks. Pressure built behind my eyes and my throat felt like the time I'd accidently swallowed a cherry pit. My vision blurred and before I knew it a tear escaped. And another. I brushed them away with a shaky hand, trying to keep it together.

"You guys—" My throat went tight as more tears fell. I was overwhelmed by their friendship.

"This feels like a group hug moment, only we don't have time," Bhakti said. "We've got to fix this. Whoever had access to your diary helped make the fake video. We know none of us told anyone about your video diary. Did you mention it to anyone else?"

"No. No one." I leaned against the wall, and slid down until I was sitting on the floor. "I think I'm going to have to suck it up and take the blame."

Shani frowned.

"That stinks," Mari grumbled.

Bhakti huffed out a sigh.

"This is so not fair." Gaby slapped her hand on the bed.

We got quiet. What else was there to say?

Except for Rowena. Ro sat hunched over her phone watching some video.

"Rowena!" Mari said. "If you're watching last week's episode of *The Voice* while we're trying to help Ali I will be most perturbed at you. Especially because we're supposed to watch it together."

"Not *The Voice*," Ro said without taking her attention from her phone. "I'm watching Ali's video. Someone posted it online."

Ugh.

"Why? Why would you watch it?" Shani sounded mad. That giiirrrl had my back.

"So I can take a screenshot of the photo. I thought there

might be a clue about who the goons are." Ro held her phone up and we all moved in to look. "But the background is too blurry which sucks because the camera caught their car."

"I appreciate it, Ro." I sent her a smile. "It's okay. Honestly. Actually, I'm okay with how this has turned out."

"I'm not," Shani said. "I'm pissed that Dax broke up with you."

"Yep. He did. And I'm going to be fine. I won't pretend I didn't like him a lot, because I did. The way I see it, maybe he didn't deserve me."

"Amen, sister." Gaby pointed at me.

"I think it's horribly unfair that the whole school hates you," Bhakti said.

"Still okay," I said. I looked around at each of their faces, thanking my lucky stars for them. "Because I've got you guys: the best friends in the world."

"Awww, you're going to make me cry." Mari sniffed. "Now it's time for a group hug!"

We did. We joined into a huddle, with our arms wrapped around each other. All of us laughing and crying at the same time. It was everything I'd needed a year ago. There was a lot to be said for the power of friendship. For having people you could trust absolutely. Maybe even something magical about it because as we stood celebrating our bond, a thought flashed through my head like a lightning bolt.

"Hang on. Let me see that photo again."

29
WHAT DOES YOUR GUT SAY?

Dax

CLOSE TO MIDNIGHT

"Dad, got a minute?" I leaned in the open door of my dad's office, a room right off the foyer. I'd caught him just hanging up the phone. He was a former Air Force pilot turned corporate pilot; the odds were slim he'd be on the phone for work this late on a Friday night. I only needed one guess as to what the phone call was about.

"Sure. Is this about the playbook mess? I've already had calls from two other parents."

Called it.

"Yeah." I slid my gaze down to my hand, fidgeted with my keys for a moment before looking back at my dad. "If someone showed you photographic proof that someone had done something bad, but your gut instinct told you it couldn't be true... What would you do?"

My dad leaned back in his chair, taking his time before answering.

"You've always had good instincts, Dax, on the field and off. I

174

can only think of one time recently when your mom and I thought your instincts might have failed you. But only once in seventeen years is a darn good track record. So, trust your gut. Trust yourself."

"What was the one time?"

"I'll just say it involved a girl."

"A girl." Huh. Recently? There had only been two girls in my life in the past year. "Are you talking about Paige? Or Ali?"

"I think you know the answer, but what does your gut tell you?"

I loved my dad, but he could be extremely frustrating when he went Yoda on me. I sighed. "For the record, this becoming an adult thing isn't always fun."

"Welcome to the party, pal."

I turned to go, but stopped, turning back to face my dad. "Would you be disappointed if I didn't end up following in your footsteps and playing for your alma mater?"

"No. Is that what you've been thinking? That I'd be upset?"

"Yeah. We've talked about it almost as long as I've been playing football."

"Only because you said that's what you wanted. Your mom and I only want to see you happy. Happy and successful at whatever you choose." He stood, walked from behind his desk, and put his hand on my shoulder. "You could quit playing football altogether and we wouldn't be disappointed. We don't need you to be a star quarterback. We're proud of you—who you are as a person."

The tightness in my chest eased and for the first time in over an hour it felt like I'd make it through the night without my lungs exploding from all the pressure.

"Is that what you want to do? Quit playing?" Dad asked.

"No," I said. "But I've only ever had one plan for my life. One vision. Recently someone suggested if I had options—you know, like a backup plan—it might take off some of the stress."

One short knock on the front door had me swinging around as TJ entered carrying a pizza from Leroy's Pizza Palace.

"Hey, Mr. DeLeon," TJ said.

"TJ. Good game tonight," Dad said. "That catch in the third quarter was stellar."

"Thanks."

TJ's catch *had* been stellar. Especially because I'd overthrown him by a couple feet. Another thing that was weighing me down. Man, when life goes south, it does it with a bulldozer not a shovel.

"We're going to hang out by the pool," I said.

"No party I hope," he said.

"Just us." That was the point of hanging out at my house. To get away from all the gossip flying around.

I detoured to my room to change out of my suit and into jeans and a sweatshirt before heading out the back door. TJ had grabbed us sodas from the fridge and turned on the outdoor gas fireplace to offset the chilly West Texas night. We sat at the wrought iron table with the pizza box between us.

"That was a great catch, by the way. I knew it was a bad pass the second it left my hand. The loss is on me."

"First off, you aren't the only player who made mistakes tonight, so shut up. Second, maybe they were the team who got our playbook. Did you think of that?"

"Oh, I've thought of it." I grabbed a slice of pizza, polished it off, and reached for another while replaying the night through my head for only the millionth time. "Damn, TJ, I still can't believe it."

"You and everyone else on the team." TJ paused for a few bites of his own piece. He shook his head. "It's not the first time there's been cheating in high school football but…"

"But who would have thought my girlfriend would be involved?"

"Girlfriend? Pretty sure you and Ali broke up when you said you didn't believe her."

"Right." I tossed my half-finished piece back in the box, suddenly not hungry. "Ex-girlfriend. If I'd stuck to my no-girls plan this season, I might not have gotten the team into this mess. So much for a distraction-free season."

"I don't know. Until tonight, Ali was cool. Paige was a ten on the high-maintenance scale and happy to cause a scene when things didn't go her way. The word manipulative comes to mind. Ali seemed like the complete opposite. She was there for you but did her own thing too. The playbook thing is weird."

"Agree. Stealing playbooks is old school. A rival team is more likely to sneak into the bleachers during practice and videotape our plays with their cellphone."

"Exactly. Except…" TJ paused, his pizza halfway to his mouth for his next bite. "A couple guys on our team—the ones who like to smack talk—bragged about our team winning the title this year with our secret weapon, Coach D's new trick plays."

"True. I still can't help the feeling that something doesn't add up. The Ali I knew—thought I knew—would never have done it." I took a drink of my soda. "Did I ever tell you she's Coach Frost's daughter?"

TJ choked on his bite of pizza and had to pound his chest twice before he could talk. "Are you kidding me? Coach Frost? *The* Coach Frost? Then the whole thing really, really doesn't make sense."

"Tell me about it." I leaned back in my chair, throwing my head to the sky as if the universe would give me the answers I needed.

The stars reminded me of Ali. Of that night in the bed of my pick-up. It seemed like forever ago. And just yesterday. That night had changed everything between us. She'd opened up to me. *I'm not great at the trust thing. I don't trust many people.* Yet that night she'd trusted me. She let me see her vulnerability and her pain.

Then there was the night we'd sat on her porch swing talking about football. Not only did she know the game, she had respect for it. Huge admiration for her dad's career as a coach.

"Why would a girl who loves football and her dad help someone cheat like that?" I asked.

"Because she thought you were cocky and wanted to bring you down a notch?"

"Maybe when we first met, but..." Not as we got to know each other. Sure, she said my ego was inflated and might float away, but she was kidding. Right? I closed my eyes and recalled her smile and her green eyes lit with laughter.

You know me. Only you have to trust yourself to see it.

Trust myself. It was like when you yell into a cave and the echo comes back at you. Over and over. This kept coming up in my life. Trust myself on the field. Trust myself for my future. Trust my instincts about Ali, even though the photo said otherwise.

I think you know the answer, but what does your gut tell you?

Something Paige said earlier tonight ran through my brain. *You think you know someone and then they show you who they are. A person can't hide who they really are.*

Paige's smile flashed up and it clicked. That edge that I couldn't put my finger on. Her smile reminded me of the time my dad had hooked a trophy-winning largemouth bass and proudly held it up for display. Satisfaction. Like she'd baited her hook and caught the prize she was after. *A person can't hide who they really are.* Exactly.

I opened my eyes and sat up, grabbing my phone off the table. "Is it too late to call Ali, do you think?"

"Dude, it's like almost one a.m. and she's pretty pissed at you. So yes."

"Dammit. You don't think if—"

"Nope. I think you should give her at least twenty-four hours." TJ reached across and took my phone out of my hands, tossing it on the table. "Why do you want to call her anyway? There's still the ugly fact that she gave your playbook to a rival team."

"No. I'm trusting my gut and my gut says she didn't."

30

PRETTY SURE I'D PEE MY PANTS

Ali

ALMOST, LIKE, ONE A.M.

"The photo? Honest, Ali, whoever took it focused on you." Ro shook her head. "Everything else is blurry."

"Email it to me anyway. I can't believe I almost forgot about this. I've got some photo editing software on my computer from when I was on the yearbook staff at Cox." I woke up my computer and brought up my mail. I downloaded the photo so I could work with it.

"First I'll deblur and lighten the photo." Which took only seconds with the software program I had. "Then I'll use another photo app to isolate the section with his arm and the car. Zoom in and … Oh, my. Anyone else see what I see?"

"If you're talking about that 'Hillcrest Football' decal, then yes!" Gaby grinned. "And the number eighty-four under it."

"Let me bring up their roster," Ro said, her fingers flying over her phone. "Number eighty-four is Seth Turk."

"Holy heck, we've got him!" Shani's eyes sparkled with satisfaction.

"Don't get too excited," Bhakti said. "Sadly, Turk's car sitting there doesn't actually prove anything, no matter what we believe."

Nothing like a bucket of cold reality in my face but I knew Bhakti was right. I felt like a passenger in a hot air balloon free-falling to the ground. Was this my fate in life? To take the blame for others?

"We might not be able to prove it, but it's a relief knowing our team didn't lose the game because of us," Shani said.

"They lost because they got outplayed." And because Dax made a couple bad throws.

"I hate to be the one to point it out, but Jackson plays Hill-crest in the first round of the playoffs," Mari said. "This Friday."

"That was a nice ten seconds of guilt-free relief." Gah! I wanted to throw my head back and scream. "Thinking out loud... What if I went to the principal without any solid proof? Do you think they'd take it seriously?"

"I'm not sure they can do anything without any proof." Bhakti shook her head. "They might think you were trying to get yourself out of trouble. Plus, there's still your dad to worry about."

Right. It was like a punch to the heart knowing my dad would start worrying about me all over again. Just when I'd managed to get him to stop worrying.

"Seth Turk. Why does his name sound so familiar?" Shani asked. "Arrgh. Why can't I ever remember? I know I've seen his name recently!"

"Ha!" Rowena snorted. "Knowing what he's done, probably on his mug shot."

"Oh, my gosh, yes. That's it!" Shani took my place at the computer and brought up the county police department site. "Last week's police blotter."

"Why in the world were you looking at the police blotter?" I asked.

"Because it's way more fun than looking at the obituaries. Duh." Shani scrolled down the page. "There it is. Seth Turk was arrested for street racing last Friday night."

"Ha-ha, his car was impounded." Bhakti read over Shani's shoulder. "Serves him right, the big jerk."

"Right? Sorry it doesn't help, Ali." Shani sighed and clicked out of the website. "But I feel better knowing karma got him in the end."

"Impounded?" Something lightened in my chest, like a balloon expanding. "Holy cow. Is the time of the arrest listed?"

"Not the time. Just the date and location." Shani brought back up the site to the police blotter. "Friday on Cemetery Road."

"Friday! Which means before midnight." I snapped my fingers. "That's only a few minutes between putting the play-book in the trunk and getting pulled over. The jerks were probably celebrating how they were going to beat us. I'd bet the playbook is still in his trunk."

"Sorry, I'm not getting how this solves anything," Gaby said. "They still have the playbook."

"Actually, they don't. It's in the trunk. All we have to do is break into the police impound lot and steal the playbook back." Bhakti cracked her knuckles. I wasn't sure if she was nervous or warming up and ready to go.

"Um, no." Rowena chewed on her thumbnail. "That sounds like a horrible idea."

"Of course it's a horrible idea." Bhakti rolled her eyes. "Do you have a better one?"

"No. But still..."

"Let's think it through," Shani said. "First, the impound lot isn't anywhere near the police station. It's on the other side of town next to that goat rescue place."

"How would you even know that?" I asked, blinking over at her.

"I know things. Second, the security is pretty shoddy. An old chain link fence with only a rusty chain and a cheap lock on the gate."

"Gosh, I don't know." Mari twirled a lock of her long ink-black hair around her finger.

"I don't like the idea." Rowena's eyes were getting bigger and more worried by the second. "Pretty sure I'd pee my pants trying to break in."

"Speaking of peeing your pants, I should probably mention the third thing. There's a guard dog locked inside at night. A vicious, snarling, fang-toothed guard dog."

Gaby frowned. "Yeah. The more we talk about it the more my stomach hurts."

"Listen to us! This is our problem right here," Bhakti said. "We're always too timid. We back down instead of fight. It's why we lost the state team championship last year. Why we lose most of our team competitions. Are we going to be goldfish or barracudas?"

"Goldfish," Rowena whispered, looking down at her clasped hands.

"It's okay, Ro. Everyone can't be a barracuda." I sent her a wink before I even thought about it. Darn, such a Dax move. "The world needs goldfish too."

"I think Bhakti's right." Mari had her fighting face on, the one she wore when someone tossed trash on the ground or abused an animal. "If there ever was a time to fight, it's now. No one gets to set up Ali and get away with it. Now, what's our plan?"

"I've got a plan." Shani rubbed her palms together. "We put on dark clothes and go break in right now. Throw a steak with a sedative to the dog like they do in the movies, pick the lock of the trunk, grab the playbook, and run like crazy."

Huh.

"Ooorrr…," I said. "We get to the impound lot when it opens

in the morning, distract the guy in charge long enough to look in the trunk, and walk out calmly, playbook in hand, un-mauled by the killer guard dog."

"I say we go with Ali's plan," Ro said, stepping forward and holding her hand out, palm to the ground.

"Yep. Un-mauled by the killer guard dog." Gaby nodded, placing her palm on top of Ro's. "Works for me."

Mari added her hand to the stack. "Sounds good. Shani?"

"Mine sounded more fun, but fine. I'm in too."

So that was what we did. It didn't end the way we'd hoped though. Here's a quick rundown:

We got to the impound lot ten minutes before it opened. Hid behind a hedge of oleander bushes to peek through the fence while we waited. Heard the snarling dog. Got scared. Dragged our inner barracudas back. A car pulled up. Guess who? Turk. Some guy (probably Goon #2) dropped him off. We freaked out, the killer guard dog charged us, and we freaked out some more. Ran to the car. Quickly decided we'd simply follow Turk when he drove off and grab the playbook from his trunk. Or from his fat, beefy hands if necessary. Looked around. *Mari's missing!* Mari jumped in the car with the killer guard dog in her arms. *Eeek!* Ro peed her pants. We were all "OMG, Mari! You stole the dog?" Mari was all "I didn't steal it. I rescued it. Poor thing had a huge chain around its neck, no water bowl, and its ribs are sticking out." Turk drove out of the lot and I fired up Milo and followed him. We ended up parked one house down from his. Turk got out of his car, caressed the front hood (not kidding), ripped a huge fart (gross!) and went inside his house.

Phew! Are you with me?

This was where we made our move. We sneaked to his car— which he'd left unlocked—opened the trunk and—

31

AS WELCOME AS A WEDGIE ON A FIVE-MILE RUN

Ali

"It's empty." By empty, I meant completely. Like Turk's head where his brain should be.

"What idiot doesn't carry a spare, a jack, and roadside flares?"

"Sort of not the point, Bhakti."

"Right. No playbook."

All six of us stood looking down into the void, hope draining from our brave barracuda hearts. Even the "killer" guard dog tucked under Mari's arm—turned out it was an ornery Chihuahua with an overbite and a loud bark—whined.

"Well, look who it is." The voice oozed from behind us, sugary-sweet and dipped in a coating of tart smugness.

Oh, man, I knew that voice. It was about as welcome as a wedgie on a five-mile run. We turned as a unit, readying to deal with the devil.

"Gosh, I wonder what y'all could be looking for." Paige stood next to Turk on his front porch. A wide, toothy smile staked out on her face.

"You know exactly what," I said, crossing my arms over my chest. "Considering you set me up."

"That's a nasty accusation, Frosty. Of course, you have evidence to back it up." She smirked. "You do, don't you? Because otherwise it's your word against mine. Oh, and the photo catching you in the act."

"How did you get it out of the trunk?" Gaby asked. "His car's been locked up all week."

"I'm sure I don't know what you're talking about." Paige descended the porch steps and stalked closer. Close enough so we could look into her pretty, blue, weasely eyes. "But I was worried that Turk would get behind on his homework, so I sweet-talked the old guy at the impound lot into letting me get his textbooks from the trunk. A pure and selfless gesture on my part for a dear friend."

Shani burst out laughing. She laughed so hard she had to grab onto my shoulder. "I'm sorry! That's the funniest thing I've ever heard. Paige Smith, pure and selfless. Ahh ha ha."

Mari snickered and Gaby tried to smother her laugh so it came out like a snort.

"Look at you and your loser friends. I guess you had to dig deep to find anyone willing to be friends with you." Paige's gaze raked over my friends like they were cellulite on her thighs. "A bunch of nobodies no one cares about. No one at school even knows you exist."

"We're not losers!" Rowena said, her voice firm. She stepped forward, into Paige's space. "We're not nobodies. My name is Rowena Clark. Remember it because I plan to help expose you for the mean, snotty, dishonest b-bitch that you are."

Go, Ro. Fierce Rowena was awesome to watch. Somewhere in the last twenty-four hours Rowena had made a trip to Emerald City. I guess we all did.

"You tell her, Ro," Gaby said.

Paige's lips pressed into a straight line and her face flushed, not in a delicate pretty way. She drew in an audible breath and sliced her gaze over to me.

"I tried to be nice to you, Frosty. If you recall, I even gave you some friendly advice." She shook her head and actually tsk-tsk'ed me. Go ahead and roll your eyes. I did. "I gave you a chance, but you ignored me. It's considered rude to walk into someone else's house and take something that belongs to someone else.

"Although..." Paige smirked and went for the jugular. "I shouldn't be surprised. Like mother like daughter."

All the anger I'd shoved deep and locked away since my mom's affair exploded out and I lunged at her. Thankfully my friends grabbed me and held me back. I'm not a pacifist, but I believed violence should be saved for only the most necessary times.

Even with all her vindictive, dirty, lowdown scheming, Paige wasn't worth it. So I didn't pull a hunk of shiny, perfectly-conditioned blond hair off her head, but I did have fun imagining it.

"I'm good now," I said, nodding a thanks to my friends for the save as they let me go. I smoothed my T-shirt down and channeled my nana. *Consider the source and ignore it.* Exactly right, Nana. "The thing is, high school is going to end. We'll be free of snotty, judgmental attitudes like yours. But you? You can't escape because you'll always be you."

Paige's face went stiff and snarly. Like her ugly personality had clawed its way through her pretty Barbie Doll shell. But she hid it quickly, letting her lips curl into a slow smile. "How's your boyfriend, Frosty? Oh, that's right, he broke up with you in front of everyone last night. How sad. Here's my last piece of advice: if you're hoping you two might kiss and make up... Don't. I know Dax. He hates to lose. When he loses the playoff game, he'll never forgive you."

I shrugged, ignoring the stabbing feeling deep in my chest.

"The joke's on you, Paige, because I don't care. I don't need his forgiveness."

That was the truth. Sure, I'd messed up—maybe even messed up big—but he hadn't even given me the chance to explain. I could pretend all I wanted that it hadn't hurt. That I'd be fine. But it had hurt. It still hurt. I was pretty sure I wouldn't forgive him either.

32

TRYING TO HUG A PRICKLY CACTUS

Dax

ALI'S HOUSE, SATURDAY, 6:48 P.M.

Standing in Ali's foyer while Coach Frost stared me down had me sweating. I'd waited twenty-four hours to talk to Ali. Okay, more like seventeen hours and forty-eight minutes. I'd followed TJ's advice to wait to give Ali a chance to cool off, but I'd failed to calculate how long a protective father would need.

"Sir, I know I made a mistake. I'd like to speak with Ali and fix it."

He gave me a piercing look before calling out, "Ali! Dax is here to see you!"

There was a long stretch of silence—so long I was afraid she'd refuse—and then she came around the corner to stand stiffly next to her dad.

Damn, she looked pretty. She didn't look mad, and that had me worried. She looked cool and disinterested. Unapproachable. Not a good sign.

"I'm going to clear out so the two of you can talk this out."

"No, Dad, don't go. I'd rather you stay," Ali said. "This won't take long since Dax and I don't have anything to talk out. Dax communicated everything very clearly last night. Crystal clear."

"Ooookay." Coach shoved his hands into his jean pockets, leaned his shoulder against the opening into the living room, and threw me a look that said, *Good luck, buddy. You're going to need it.*

I focused on Ali, hating the distance between us. The emotional distance. Ali was back into that loner, protective mode like when I first met her. Cracking through that tough shell hadn't been easy the first time. It felt like a gut punch realizing I might not break through a second time. I sucked in a breath and tried anyway.

"You were right. You told me I knew you, only I had to trust myself to see it. I do know you. I know whatever happened, it wasn't to hurt me or the team. You've shown me in so many ways who you are. You're smart, honest, authentic, generous and brave."

"Darn, DeLeon, according to you I'm a Girl Scout," she said, arms across her chest and not even a smidge of a smile on her lips.

"Not hardly. Sometimes your honesty cuts like a scalpel, you can be stubbornly independent, and getting to know you was like trying to hug a prickly cactus. Is that better?"

Coach Frost cleared his throat and shook me off with a subtle head shake.

"What I'm trying to say, Ali, is I'm sorry. I wish I had a do-over. I was an idiot—"

"Oh, hey, look. We agree on something." Still no softening from Ali.

"Okay, well, obviously you aren't ready to forgive me. Which I get. I want you to know, even though I don't know what went down, I know it wasn't you."

Ali didn't say anything, but gave me a curt nod of her head.

"My gut—which I wish I'd listened to last night—tells me Paige is involved in this somehow. Which means this whole thing—you getting blamed and everyone in school…"

"Hating me?"

"Right. It's my fault." I didn't care that Ali was strong enough to handle being the most hated girl in school a second time. Because I wasn't going to let her. I would find a way to fix it. "Would you be willing to tell me what really happened? Not because I need proof. But I'd like to see where Paige fits in so I can try to fix this."

"Honestly, it doesn't matter how it happened," she said. "It's done. You should probably spend your time figuring out how you're going to approach your playoff game now that the other team has all your plays."

Yeah. Coach Devlin's special plays that were going to give us the edge and hopefully lead us to the championship. I didn't have a solution for that other than we'd have to play a hell of a game.

"They stole your playbook?" Coach Frost asked, sounding more coach than worried father suddenly.

"I gave it to them," Ali said, her gaze still on mine.

"What the heck, Ali?" He was full on angry Coach Frost now.

"Coach, she didn't," I said without a doubt in my mind.

"I did." She closed her eyes and blew out a breath before turning to look at her dad. "I stole Dax's playbook and gave it to the other team."

"There's a lot more to the story," I said.

"As both a father and a coach…" His voice was scary-serious, like get down and give me fifty up-downs serious. "…I'd like to hear it. The whole story. In fact, let's go sit."

Coach led the way into his office and took a seat at his desk. Ali sagged down on one of the two over-stuffed chairs facing him and I took the other.

She narrowed her gaze on me and huffed out a breath. "Fine. It all started when I agreed to be Dax's fake girlfriend—"

"Excuse me?" Her dad's gaze sliced over to me.

"Dad, I'll never get through the story if you interrupt me every time you hear something crazy. This story is chock full of crazy."

"Sorry. I'll shut up. Although, Dax, you and I will be having a talk later, but I'll shut up and listen." He frowned at me before turning back to Ali. "So you agreed to be Dax's pretend girlfriend...?"

Great. I'd pissed off Coach Frost. Should be a fun talk. Maybe he'd let me do those fifty up-downs instead.

The story Ali proceeded to tell *was* full of crazy. It started when she was jumped in Bowl-O-Rama's parking lot by goons demanding a playbook. The goons poured a milkshake in her bowling ball and threatened her before running off. And the crazy kept going: Mr. and Ms. Jackalope were kidnapped, Ali found a ransom note in her locker, the fake playbook Ali and her friends tried to swap for the rabbits, a second ransom note with a fake bloody rabbit's foot, and stealing my playbook from my truck so they could get Mr. and Ms. Jackalope back. Finally ending at the big finale: the doctored video to make Ali look guilty.

Holy crap.

"Is that it?" her dad asked.

"Except for the part where the person I thought knew me and trusted me believed I could do something like that and publicly dumped me."

"Ali—" I started, but she cut me off.

"Oh, wait. There is more. Last night, when my friends came over—friends who actually trusted me and believed me, just sayin'—we figured out who the goon was. I'm not going to name him since I have no proof. He isn't on a team you've played so far." Ali glanced at me, and shrugged. "Sorry, but you lost Friday's game on your own without help from me."

"Ali...," her dad said, sending me an apologetic glance.

"Like I said, surgical precision." I winked at her. Considering her face stiffened up and she looked like she was figuring out how to remove a vital organ or two with that scalpel, in retrospect, the wink had been a bad move.

33

GONNA NEED A HAIL MARY PASS

Dax

ON ALI'S SHIT LIST, 7:15 P.M.

"Dad? Will you please tell DeLeon that if he winks at me one more time, I'm going to use one of those moves you taught me?"

"Ixnay the winking, Dax." Coach shot me a don't-poke-the-bear look before turning back to Ali. "Keep going. What about the goon and the playbook?"

"The goon's car got impounded about ten minutes after I gave them the playbook. So, we came up with a plan to steal the playbook back while his car was locked up."

"Tell me you didn't break in to the impound lot," her dad said.

"No! I mean, we thought about it, but no. We went there this morning right when it opened. Except the goon was there too to pick up his car." Ali frowned and shook her head, clearly frustrated with the guy. "We followed him, thinking we'd retrieve it when he went into his house. Only the playbook wasn't there. And then Paige showed up."

Coach Frost sat back in his chair looking a bit shell-shocked. "Well, you weren't kidding. That's a crazy story."

"We also sort of rescued the guard dog from the impound lot," Ali mumbled. "Technically, I guess we stole it, in case the police call you along with Principal Barstow."

"Paige set you up because of me. She was angry that you and I were together," I said. "She's the one who doctored your video."

"Yeah, I still haven't figured out how she accessed my private V-log, but yes."

"Your phone. One day at bowling, while you were at the shoe counter talking with Mr. J, she handed me your phone and said you must have dropped it."

"She's a peach, that one. You sure can pick 'em. Anyway..." Ali slapped her hands on her thighs. "That's where we are. Paige gave the playbook back to the goon, and you're playing against them in the first playoff game. So if you lose, everyone really *can* blame me for the loss."

"Not you." I leaned forward, resting my elbows on my knees. "Paige and that cheating jerk."

"Thanks to the video and the photo, everyone thinks it's all on me. No one's going to believe I had good intentions or that Paige set me up."

"Ali, honey, why didn't you come to me for help? You know I've got connections."

"Dad, you quit your job for me because I worried you so much." She blinked at him, her eyes tearing up. "There was no way I was going to put you through that again. Plus, you promised that after you saw I was okay, you'd start living again. So I threw myself into showing you I was okay. I made friends and ogled cute boys. That's why I agreed to fake-dating Dax."

"So none of it was real?" he asked.

"Not in the beginning. The funny thing is, it grew into the real thing. I love my bowling teammates. They're the best friends a girl could have. The thing with Dax..." Ali looked at me and the sadness shining in her eyes reached out and wrapped a tight fist around my throat.

"What we had was real too. *Is* real," I said. "Only I screwed up."

"Back to the playoff game," Ali said. "I feel horrible that Jackson might lose."

"So we won't lose," I said. "We'll simply have to outplay them."

"You guys are good," Ali said. "But so is the other team. The fact that they know your plays, gives them the edge."

"Maybe not..." Coach pulled open his desk drawer, grabbed out a playbook, and handed it to me. "This might help."

I stared down at my hands. I was holding the Holy Grail of playbooks. "You'd let us use your plays?"

"Absolutely. As a coach there are three things I can't stand: laziness, bad sportsmanship, and cheating. They cheated. I'm only helping level the playing field."

"Wow. I can't thank you enough, Coach. This is amazing." I flipped through some pages, shaking my head. "Your playbook is legendary."

"Will you have enough time to learn them?" Ali asked.

"Sure." I nodded. "We only need two or three good new plays."

"That's exactly right," Coach agreed. "Plus, you'll have the advantage of surprise on your side."

Coach and I grinned at each other.

"Okay then. I'll leave you two to talk football." Ali stood abruptly and left the room without even a backward glance.

I stared after her, regretting I was such an idiot.

"She is royally pissed at you," Coach said.

"Tell me about it." I looked across at him. "Do you think she'll ever forgive me?"

"I don't know. Getting hurt by people she trusted—that's still an open wound." His face said it would be a long shot. "A deep wound, so forgiveness won't be easy. Maybe give her some space for a few days."

Space. I could try. We had bowling class together, but I could keep quiet and let her bowl.

"And...I think you're going to have to come up with a Hail Mary pass."

A Hail Mary pass: a pass made in desperation with only a small chance of success.

"Yeah, I'm afraid you're right." The thing about a Hail Mary pass was—you only had one shot at it.

34

ALI AND THE TERRIBLE, HORRIBLE, NO GOOD, VERY BAD WEEK

Ali

SCHOOL PARKING LOT, MONDAY MORNING

After a short reprieve from the Thanksgiving break—Dad and I ate a quiet Thanksgiving meal at the Bluebird Diner—it was back to school and time to face reality. The false hope that time might have lessened the gossip and the anger was quickly dashed.

I pulled into the student parking lot Monday morning to find someone had been nice enough to decorate my parking spot. They'd spray-painted some clever, bordering on inspiring, sobriquets for me in large, white letters. *Sweet.* I parked, shut off my engine—one, two, moo—and sat in my car, waiting for the bell to ring.

Grabbing my phone from my backpack on the seat next to me, I clicked on my video to record this super-duper moment for posterity.

"All right, Ali—Oh! And anyone else who's enjoying watching my private diary—you already know this week at school is going to be the most amazing, fantastic, and super-

awesome week ever. The fun nicknames, notes of encouragement in my locker, the shower of confetti tossed at me in class,
and the enthusiastic supportive pats on the back in the hallways.
So. Much. Fun. Who wouldn't want to be me? Today's objective:
exchange oxygen and CO_2 like a boss. Positive affirmation: I am
a diamond. I shine under pressure."

The bell rang and I headed to the activity bus.

"Traitor!" some kid yelled across the parking lot.

"You don't belong here, loser!" someone else bellowed.

I lifted my chin higher and stepped onto the bus to a
greeting of boos.

You know what? Instead of dragging you through this, I'll
glide over a few details. The rest of the day went exactly how
you'd think it went. It was pretty much Groundhog Day the rest
of the week. Remember when I said I'd never be chum again?
Wrong again, Ali Frost. I was chum. I was the weakest gazelle on
the tundra. I was the rabbit caught out in the open. Almost
exactly like what happened at Cox.

I say almost because there was one huge I'm-a-lucky-girl
difference. This time I had rock-solid friends who stood by me.
They took flak for defending me, but they didn't back down.
Shani, Gaby, Mari, Rowena, and Bhakti were fiercely protective.
They were barracudas.

Dax kept his distance, even in bowling class. He was polite
and friendly, yet didn't press me for conversation. Maybe he
was distracted with football—learning the new plays for the
playoff game. Or maybe he didn't care anymore. Had he moved
on? Maybe. Except something in his eyes said maybe not. Those
dark fathomless eyes of his still held heat, interest, and intensity
when his gaze met mine.

Either way, I was not going to obsess about Dax's hot gaze. It
didn't matter. I was over Dax. No, that was a lie. But I was
trying to get over him. Trying to ignore the way Paige and
Gwen flirted with him in bowling class. I kept my focus on the

lane stretched out in front of me and not on the way Paige touched Dax's wrist or grabbed onto his biceps or ran her gaze over him like he was completely edible and she was on another grapefruit diet. Nope. Didn't notice any of that.

The highlight of the week was our last regular season bowling competition on Thursday.

We stood in a circle, our hands piled on top of each other's, ready for our pre-competition cheer. Only things were different now.

"Ro, I can still see your face when you stood up to Paige and called her a 'mean, snotty, dishonest bitch.' All this week you guys have had my back. You've been ferocious, bold, and undaunted in the face of all the ugliness this week. You know what that means?"

"We're freaking barracudas," Shani said.

"Yeah, we are." Rowena nodded once, her lips sliding into a huge, cheesy grin.

Then we were all grinning.

"We've never won the team competition," Mari said. "I say that changes today."

"Let's do this," Bhakti said. "Make every roll count. Balls to the wall."

"Um, you mean that metaphorically, right?" Gaby asked. "Not literally."

"Whatever it takes," I said, more fired up to bowl than I can remember. This felt bigger than the state championships even. "Barracudas on three. One. Two. Three."

"Barracudas!" We shouted and blew up our hand stack.

Someone snorted from three lanes over. I turned to look. *Figures.* Kayla Tercera, aka Snotty Gold Shoes.

"You do know you guys are those imaginary rabbits, right?" Tercera smirked.

"Not today," Mari said.

My dad arrived and handed me a colorful bouquet of wildflowers which made my whole team ooh and ah.

"Holy cupcake, Coach Frost! That is so sweet," Gaby said.

"They're not from me," he said. "They're from Dax."

Even more oohs and ahs from my friends.

Part of me wished I was strong enough to toss them in the trash can.

Dad must have seen that thought flash across my face because he grabbed my hand. "I know it hurt, kiddo, but he did apologize and believe you before he knew the details. That's something."

He gave me a wink and walked off to talk with Mr. J until we got underway.

"Not that you asked for my opinion, but I think Dax is a good guy who made a mistake." Bhakti wrapped her arm around my shoulders. "I think you should give him a second chance."

"I agree. I like Dax," Gaby said. "I like how much you smiled when you and Dax were together."

I shook my head. "I thought he knew me, but he didn't."

"He made a mistake." Shani tilted her head, arching an eyebrow in my direction. "I sort of remember your knee-jerk reaction when someone accessed your video diary. There were a few seconds when you thought it could be one of us."

Rowena nodded her agreement.

"A few seconds when you didn't trust us," Mari said, wrapping her arm around my waist on my other side. "We understood that it was a gut reaction in a moment of pain. We forgave you."

We forgave you. They had.

"You don't have to decide right now. In fact, you shouldn't." Gaby steered me back over to our assigned lanes. "No more thinking about Dax until we're at the game tomorrow night."

"Wait, what? No, I'm not going—"

"Yes, you are," Shani said and every one of them nodded. "We're going together. You're going to show Paige that she didn't win. Now, speaking of winning... Let's roll, bitches."

We threw ourselves into the team competition like never before. Each of us reached deep for every roll.

"Are you ready to be out-bowled, Jackalopes?" Undaunted in the face of Tercera's smack talk and her gold shoes. "We don't even have to try hard; your team chokes. Every. Time."

"Tercera, none of us want your opinion," I said. "Would it kill you to be a good sport?"

"Fine. Good luck." And then she ruined it with a smirk. "You'll need it because, just like last time, we're taking the trophy home."

We were bold, going hard on every strike and spare.

"Hey, no hard feelings when we beat you." Tercera smirked. "Someone's got to finish second."

We were ferocious.

"The object of the game is to knock down the pins, sweetie." Tercera's disingenuous advice rolled off our backs.

Frame by frame, Tercera and her team got quieter. Their puffed-up confidence deflated as our team matched them roll by roll.

Shani, Gaby, Mari, and Bhakti rolled their highest scores ever in a competition. Rowena was awful close. Our team didn't have a single foul or gutter ball. We set a team record for the number of spares picked up. As for me... I rolled my second 300 game. Twelve times I hit the pocket with every roll. Twelve strikes. It was important to be good sports, but our team enjoyed seeing Tercera's face pucker up like she'd sucked a lemon with each of my last three strikes.

And, okay, I might have grinned when Shani called across

the lane, "Hey, Tercera! Do they make those shoes in silver or bronze?" The girl looked close to throwing one of her gold shoes at Shani.

It really was a perfect game. I wasn't talking about me; I was talking about our team.

Coach Diamond was ecstatic. "That was some DGB, girls. Darn good bowling. You roll like that in the spring and I'll be shoving those dusty football and lacrosse trophies aside for our bowling trophy front and center in the display case."

DGB.

Yep… Darn Good Bowling.

But also… Dangerous Girl Barracudas.

35

LEVEL THE PLAYING FIELD

Dax

Friday Night, Jackson vs. Hillcrest, 7 p.m.

It was finally Friday night. I'd needed the week to slow down so we had more time to work on the new plays, but I wanted it to speed forward to get this game over with. I'd gone into games fired up before. Never like this though. We didn't simply want to win. We wanted to beat them so badly that they'd always be remembered as the team that cheated and still couldn't win.

Our whole team had thrown everything into preparing and learning Coach Frost's plays. Coach Devlin had been more than happy to use them once he'd been advised by Principal Barstow that there was a high probability his secret plays were no longer secret.

The rumor was—and I didn't hear this from Ali since she wasn't talking to me—that other than the one incriminating photo of Ali, the administration hadn't dug anything else up.

Thirty minutes to game time and our team was wrapping up our warm ups, ready to head to the locker room for our pre-game ritual. Tonight, I had a pre-game thing of my own. On our way back to the locker room, TJ gave me a nod and we peeled off onto the path toward the stands.

The cheerleaders stood around stretching and fixing their hair. People walked by to make their way to their seats. The drum line was getting the crowd juiced up with "Bula, Bula." I scoped the area, nodded to a friend, before moving next to TJ. We stood at the edge of the tunnel we'd be running out of shortly, our helmets tucked under our arms, taking it all in.

"Dax!" Paige sent me a bright smile, walking over until she stood right in front of me. Of course, Gwen trailed along too.

"Dude," TJ said, frowning at me. "Ali's here. Do you want her to see you with Paige?"

"So what? Everyone knows Ali and I are on the outs." I shrugged and locked eyes with Paige. "After what happened, well, let's just say we haven't been talking."

"I'm sorry you had to go through that, Dax. I can't believe she did what she did." Paige pouted and gave my forearm a squeeze. "I'm still shocked at the lengths she went to. So devious."

"I'll be honest…at one point I thought maybe you did it."

"*What?*" Her eyes went wide.

"I thought maybe you were trying to get us back together. The idea blew me away." I smoothed a piece of blond hair off her face. "It's a powerful thing to think someone likes you that much. It made me remember what we had. What it was like between us… And I got this feeling in my chest."

"You did?" She blinked up at me, her lips tilting up in a tentative smile.

"I did. When I found out it was Ali, the disappointment hit me hard. Part of me wished it had been you. Trying to get me back."

"It was her!" Gwen said, her voice bubbling and giggly. "She does want you back!"

"Shut up, Gwen," Paige hissed, throwing a quick frown at her friend. "Don't listen to her. She's—"

I placed a finger gently on her lips. "It's okay, Paige. Like I said, it goes to a guy's head. It makes me rethink everything."

"Everything?"

"Pretty much. So if stealing the playbook was your idea, you should take credit. I'm not lying when I say no other girl has made me feel the way you do." I took her hands in mine and looked hard into her eyes. "I'm amazed at the lengths you went to, trying to get us back together."

"I—I did do it. It was my idea to steal the playbook. I came up with the whole plan. I missed you so much, Dax. I knew our break up had been a mistake." Paige flashed me her big cheerleader smile. "You really remembered what we had?"

"I did. Remembering what we had dug up all the memories… Of how selfish you are. How everything revolves around you. I remembered you can be meaner than a junkyard dog, thinking nothing of ripping someone down to nothing. Yeah, and the feeling in my chest was heartburn."

"Wait, what?"

I turned and looked over my shoulder. "You get all that?"

"Every word." TJ lowered his phone, turning to the girl next to him. "Rowena? Did you get the feed?"

"Uploading it now." The iPad in Rowena's hands was connected to TJ's phone. "It should play in four…three…two…one."

Right on cue, Paige's face filled up the video scoreboard at the end of the field. Since Paige had aired the footage of Ali handing off the playbook to the whole school, it seemed like airing her confession was the best way to stomp the lie out.

Paige may be the prettiest girl in school on the outside, but she was one of the ugliest inside where it really counted.

"Oh my God." Paige gasped. Her face paled and her eyes went wide with shock. "I can't believe you did this."

"I didn't. You did. You did this to yourself and now everyone knows." I turned away, not caring what the fallout for Paige would be. She'd earned everything that was coming her way. If the boos in the stands were anything to go by, she'd get an earful. I nodded to Rowena. "Thanks."

"Are you kidding? It was my pleasure. No one messes with a bowling teammate and gets away with it."

"Hey, hotshot." TJ lifted his chin to me. "We've been gone for over five minutes. Let's get back to the team."

"Absolutely. We've got a game to win."

Hillcrest won the coin toss and chose to receive first. I stood on the sidelines between TJ and Grady while our defense got things rolling. Our team was extra fired up. No one should be able to cheat their way into the championship game.

We kicked the ball and their receiver caught it on the twenty-six yard line and took off. Josh brought him down on the thirty-one. Not great, but I'd chalk it up to opening jitters. Sure enough, our defense settled down and held them to a field goal.

Coach Devlin grabbed my shoulder. "Calm and steady, Dax. Start with blue left, 27 Z-in."

I ran onto the field and into the huddle. "Blue left, 27 Z-in, on one, on one. Ready, break."

Everyone clapped and we formed up and got down to business. Our teams were evenly matched so the first half was spent trading scores. With five minutes to go in the first half, it was fair to say everyone on the field was tense and anxious.

With the goal of running into the locker room at halftime with a lead, we tried one of Coach Devlin's plays, the mad steer. Hillcrest shut it down like they knew it was coming. Because, of course, they did.

Two of Hillcrest's defensive backs grinned at me like monkeys on acid.

Just as the whistle blew signaling half-time, one of them called to me.

"Hey, DeLeon! Tell your girlfriend thanks...for the book loan." His smirk spread wider across his face. "Oh, did that shock you? Hahaha."

"Yeah." I pulled off my helmet and walked toward him. "I'm shocked you know how to read."

"You calling me stupid?" He strode forward, getting in my face, along with the rest of their defensive line.

"I guess that depends," I said, sensing some of my teammates joining me. "See, my girlfriend never revealed your name since she didn't have proof. But now we do because you just gave it to me. Does that qualify as stupid?"

Instant scrum on the fifty-yard line. There was pushing, name calling, and maybe even a few punches landed before the referees busted it up and our coaches wrangled us off into the locker rooms.

"Totally figures it was Turk. The guy's always been a jerk," Grady said on our way in. "Should we tell Coach?"

"Absolutely. After the game," TJ said. "After we humiliate him on the field."

"My thinking exactly." TJ and I locked gazes. "Let's make sure Turk feels how much he's motivated our team."

36

ESCAPING FROM QUICKSAND

Dax

HALFTIME

"Was that anything I need to know about, Dax?" Coach Devlin asked.

"No, Coach."

He gave me a long look before nodding. "Okay, guys. Grab some water and listen up. Hillcrest is good, but we're better. They're overconfident. We're determined. Dirty tricks won't help them. We'll beat them playing a clean game. With our new plays, we've got the element of surprise on our side. Defense, keep it up. Railes, awesome job. We're going to run as much as we can third quarter, then open up our passing game in the fourth. Captains?"

"Oh, yeah," TJ said, standing up on a bench. "Anyone who has a chance to tackle number 84 and misses has to buy Josh lunch at the Burger Barn."

Laughter, groans, and cat-calls filled the room. Everyone knew that wouldn't be cheap as Josh could put down four burgers in fifteen minutes.

"Clean hits, guys, but don't let up," I added, moving next to TJ and sticking my hand out into the center of the circle. "Let's do this. Jackalopes on three."

Everyone drew in, adding their hands to the pile. "One, two, Jackalopes!"

Third quarter was all defense with neither team scoring. You can believe our offensive line was sharp. They missed no tackles. Not once did Turk make it through. He might have even eaten dirt a couple of times.

The tension ramped up heading into the fourth quarter. After a whole season, twelve minutes would decide if we'd make it back to the championship game.

Twelve minutes. We were running out of time to make something happen. Adrenaline rushed through my body like five energy drinks injected into my veins.

We huddled. "TJ, they're all over you. Wing T 69 bootleg right on one." TJ, Grady, and Jake broke away. "Wing T 69 bootleg right on one. On one."

We clapped and took our positions.

Jake hiked me the ball. I took two steps, faked a handoff to Smith, and rolled right while I checked my receivers. Grady had a defender matching him step for step. Should I throw to TJ instead? Shit, they had him double covered. *Throw the dang ball, idiot.* I threw a bomb down field to Grady, but my hesitation threw the timing off. Grady hurled himself in the air almost making a spectacular catch. Almost. He managed to get his fingertips on it, tipping it right into the cornerback's hands.

Interception.

Damn it. I tore my helmet off on my way to the sidelines. Grabbing a cup of Gatorade, I paced behind the bench, trying to pull it together. What was I doing?

Double damn. I had one foot in quicksand. A glance at the

field—just in time to see Hillcrest get a first down on our forty-nine—had me slipping more. Tumbling in. It felt like a giant hand clenched around my chest. I grabbed another Gatorade and paced some more.

"Dax, shake it off, man," TJ said. "Get out of your head."

I stopped in front of TJ and sucked air into my lungs. Right. Get out of my head. Positive thoughts. I sorted through all my positive mantras for one I could grab onto to pull myself out of the negative spiral.

"I need to stop second-guessing myself," I said. *It was a stupid throw.*

"It's just a game." *Was this going to be a repeat of last year's championship game?*

Nothing was working. I closed my eyes and cleared my mind. That's when I heard Ali's voice… *"Nana Frost used to say, 'When you think things are bad and getting worse, ask yourself… What's the worst that can happen?'"*

"Right. What's the worst that can happen?" I asked, trying to talk myself through this.

"You mean other than we lose?"

"Yeah, what else?"

"I don't see how this is helpful." TJ crushed his empty cup and threw a frown at me. "What else is there? We lose. No chance at the state title."

"Work with me here, TJ. We lose. No championship game. I don't impress the scouts. I don't get a scholarship. I don't get into Tech—or any other four-year college… That's all." I stared into TJ's eyes as the hand around my chest relaxed and I took a steady breath.

"What the hell do you mean 'that's all'?"

"I can go to community college. Or Ali and I can be welders together." I grinned.

"Did you take a hit to your head?" he asked, looking confused as heck. "Since when did you want to be a welder?"

"Since never. Damn, TJ, it's like you don't know me." I looked over TJ's shoulder to see that Hillcrest was now on our nine. Second and nine. Easily within touchdown or field goal range. "What else if I lose the game?"

"*What else?* I don't know! You'll be a failed QB and all the girls at school will stop drooling over you." He leaned in, looking closer into my eyes. "I should tell Coach you've got a concussion."

"Ali will. She likes me for who I am." *You don't have to prove yourself out on that field. Not to me. A loss doesn't dent your armor. You're smart and nice and funny.* Remembering Ali's words made me smile, but then I remembered how pissed she was at me and that wiped the smile off my face. "I mean, she's not too thrilled with me right now, but that has nothing to do with losing. What else?"

"What the hell is your point?" TJ threw his arms in the air. "I have no friggen idea, Dax. You tell me. What else will happen?"

"Nothing." I grinned, moving my gaze back to the field.

Vasquez forced the QB to fumble and Kalvecky recovered and ran it to the thirty-one before someone brought him down. Thanks to our defense, Hillcrest didn't capitalize on my mistake.

"Way to go!" I yelled. Sliding my helmet back on, I smiled at TJ. "Let's go have some fun."

"Dax!" Coach called as I fist bumped our defense on their way by me.

"I've got this!" I ran onto the field, a plan forming in my head with every step. "Huddle up!"

First and ten. "Parker, you're taking it straight up the middle."

"That hasn't worked all game," Parker said.

I gave him a sharp look. "That's the play. Loose Red 34 zone blast. On one, on one."

Jake hiked the ball, I handed it off to Parker and just like he'd said, it didn't work. One measly yard.

Second and nine. "Okay, we're trying the mad steer again."

"Dude, Coach D's play didn't work. They're ready for it."

"I'm asking you to trust me. Mad steer, on two, on two. Break."

There was a bit of grumbling and frustrated looks but we ran the mad steer. Hillcrest shut it down, smirking and smack talking.

Third and nine. This time there was ugly tension in the huddle.

"What in the actual hell, Dax?" Grady growled. "Are you trying to throw this game along with your girlfriend?"

I grabbed Grady by the front of his jersey pulling him close so we stood face mask to face mask. "Ali was set up. I'm trying to win." I let him go and looked around the huddle at all the doubting and confused faces. "Okay, that was the set-up. Here's the payoff. Hercules, on one."

"One of Coach Frost's plays." TJ didn't smile, but his eyes lit up and he gave me a nod. "Excellent."

"Hercules, on one, on one. Break." We clapped and took our positions.

Jake hiked the ball, I fell back, faked a hand-off to Parker, lateraled over to TJ who ran five yards, cut left and passed it downfield to Grady who sailed into the end zone.

Touchdown! Yes! I pointed at my offensive line and then over to TJ while Grady did the sprinkler dance. The extra point had us up 21-14.

Our defense held Hillcrest to a field goal in the fourth. We added another touchdown with one more of Coach Frost's plays, got the extra point, and won the game 28-17. Championship bound.

We celebrated on the sidelines. I tore off my helmet, turning when my dad called my name. He and mom gave me two thumbs up and beaming smiles.

Coach D clapped me on the shoulder. "Dax, that was some gutsy play calling."

"Thanks, Coach." I hadn't felt this good after a win since last season. I'd missed this walking-on-air feeling.

"You did *not* just do that!" TJ grabbed me in a bear hug, smacking me on the back. "I thought you'd lost it over on the sidelines. Tell Ali to thank her dad for us."

"If I can ever get her to talk to me, you bet." The reminder that Ali and I weren't together, let alone talking, was like a punch in the gut.

TJ grinned. "Yeah, I don't think that's going to be a problem."

"You didn't see her face the last time we talked," I said with a grimace.

"True. But I can see her face right now, and…well, have a look for yourself." TJ grabbed my shoulders and spun me around to face the bleachers.

I stood there staring at the most beautiful sight. Maybe I did believe in luck after all. Because Ali stood in the bleachers looking at me with the sweetest smile on her face. She was bundled up in her over-sized, old Army jacket and her red curls were loose, blowing about her face. Just when I thought there couldn't be anything better—Ali opened her jacket wide.

Aw, hell yes.

Ali Frost was wearing my jersey.

37

BOWLING BOYFRIEND
(NOW A THING!)

Ali

If I had dreamed Dax's reaction to seeing me in his jersey, I couldn't have dreamed anything better than real life. He stood still and took me in with his intense gaze while his teammates celebrated with body slams and high fives around him. And then the too hot, up-to-no good, very beastly boy grinned. His grin slid into a wide smile as he strode toward me, eating up ground with his long strides.

I hurried down the bleachers to meet him.

When we stood only feet apart, the crowd disappeared and it was only Dax and me and electrified air between us.

"I...I don't even know where to start," I said. There was the bouquet of flowers, Paige's public confession, the whole game—that amazing fourth quarter!—and the win.

"I do. Right here." He cupped my face and kissed me.

He was hot, sweaty, and covered in dirt and it was perfect. It was a long, slow kiss that said I'm sorry and never again, and he wrapped his arm around me tight saying *that's my girl*. I threw my arms around his neck because Dax DeLeon was my guy and I wanted everyone to know.

When we pulled apart, I stood breathless and lightheaded, gazing up into his eyes. We both started talking at once.

"I'm sorry—"

"I'm sorry—"

"You go first," he said.

"I'm sorry about the whole mess. I wish I'd figured out some other plan, but…well, I didn't."

"I'm sorry I didn't trust you—" The look of sincere pain in his eyes got to me.

"Stop it. You already apologized. I know some girls love a good grovel, but not me."

"Have I told you I'm crazy about you?" He pressed a kiss to my temple. The warmth from his lips rippled through me. "I'm sorry I missed your bowling meet. Dang, Ali, a perfect game!"

"It's okay. We've got more meets in the spring. Hey… Thank you," I said, pulling back a little to look into his eyes. "For Paige's confession. It was amazing and unexpected. I was prepared to handle the kids hating me, but—"

"—but now you don't have to."

"I have to admit, I like your way better." I felt so free. Like Dobby-free.

"Me too. There was no way I was going to stand by and let you take the fall."

"How did you get her to confess? On video, no less?"

He smiled his crooked smile. "A little bad boy charm. Rowena helped us with the video. She said, and I quote, 'No one messes with a bowling teammate and gets away with it.'"

"I'm blessed with amazing friends." My life was richer because of my friends and Dax. It was weird that my most painful experience had brought my greatest gift. Like it was meant to be. I would never in a million years have wanted my dad to go through the pain he did. But maybe—once he got back to living a real life again—maybe he'd find something wonderful and perfect too.

"Your friends are very cool."

"How did you find out Turk was the one?"

He arched an eyebrow at me. "How do you know we found out?"

"Oh please. At first I was confused when the offensive line shuffled around every play." I shook my head and laughed. "Then I realized it was so everyone got a turn at Turk. Heck, you even tackled him!"

"You bet your ass I did. He was dumb enough to tell us. Proof that Paige was the brains behind the plot because Turk would volunteer to be goalie for the dart team."

"Dax!" Dad joined us. "Great game, son. That was some play calling in the fourth quarter."

"Thanks, Coach." Dax wrapped his arm around my shoulders and pulled me against his side. "Your plays made that happen."

"The plays helped, but your execution was the key." Dad gave him one of his "I'm impressed" nods. "I was afraid you'd lose momentum after the interception, but you came back stronger."

"A little trick Ali taught me." He winked at me.

"Gutsy move, Dax." My dad laughed. "The last time you winked at her you almost lost a body part."

"We've worked it out." I turned my face up to Dax, loving the way his gaze ate me up. "I can put up with his winks."

He grinned. "Thanks, babe."

"Whoa. I'm drawing the line at babe. That's still a no."

"Gotcha, gummy bear." He winked again.

"Okaaay, well, this got weird, so I'll head out now." Dad shook Dax's hand and turned to go, only to turn back. "I sat next to Zeke Poppe, the recruiter for Texas Tech. He was impressed. Just thought I'd mention it. G'night."

I grabbed Dax's hand in mine and squeezed. "Dax, that's fantastic—"

He cut me off when he pulled me up against him, face to face. "If I get a scholarship, great. But I'll be okay if I don't. Want to know why?"

"Why?" I whispered, my heart beating faster than a bee's wing.

"Because I've got a backup plan," he said, smoothing the hair from my face. "And a girl who likes me for who I am even if I'm not a football star."

This time, I kissed him.

"Okay you two, stop with the sucking face," TJ said. I had no idea how long he'd been standing there. "We're trying to make plans. There's a bonfire at the lake or there's a party at Whelan's place. What do you want to do?"

"Actually, I'm in the mood for some midnight bowling," Dax said, raising his eyebrows at me. "What do you think? Girls against the guys? Bowlers versus the football players?"

"Absolutely, but you guys are going down," I said.

"Righteous." TJ pointed at us. "I'll tell the gang. Sorry, Ali, but we won't go easy on you because you're girls."

"Oh, TJ." I shook my head at the poor, unsuspecting jock. "If anyone's going to be crying for mercy, it'll be you namby-pamby football players. Me and my girls are sort of badass bowlers."

We all met up at Bowl-O-Rama after Dax and the guys had showered and changed. Dax and I arrived first with a gaggle of at least twenty kids not far behind us. Along with our group of bowlers and football players, there were also cheerleaders (*not* Paige and her posse), some lacrosse players, Lacey, Nathan Baker, and Kev.

Mr. J took one look at me and rolled his eyes. "Get out of here, Ali. I hate seeing you alone on a Friday night. Go. Skedaddle. Scram."

"I'm not alone. I'm with friends. And my..." Heat rushed into my cheeks, unsure of how to introduce Dax.

"She's with me, sir. Dax DeLeon." Dax stuck his hand out to shake Mr. J's. "I'm Ali's boyfriend."

"Well, okay then." Mr. J grabbed Dax's extended hand and pulled him close—as close as you could with a counter between them. "Son, you hurt her and I'll—"

"*Ahem.* Stand down, Mr. J." I shot him a warning look. Sure, I'd pretty much grown up here at Bowl-O-Rama, but I already had one overprotective father.

"You'd have to get in line behind me anyway, Mr. J," Shani said with a grin in Dax's direction.

"You guys can have lanes one through four," Mr. J said.

We spent the next hour bowling, talking and laughing, and even a little dancing behind the ball rack. Everyone was still rehashing tonight's game and getting geared up for the championship next week. There was some serious smack talk between the girls and guys teams.

At one point, TJ ended up standing next to me while everyone else watched Josh attempt to down an order of tater tots in thirty seconds.

"You look good in his jersey," he said. "Dax has had a couple girlfriends in high school, but you're the first girl who's worn his jersey. I thought you might like to know."

"Thanks, TJ." That knowledge melted me into a puddle of love-struck goo. Wow. The first and only girl to wear Dax's jersey.

Turned out all that couple stuff I'd rejected before felt... really, really good.

Was it only ten weeks ago that I'd stood in this alley and wished I could have rushed through senior year? Crazy how fast things can change. Future-me and past-me could kiss my grits, because I didn't want to be anywhere else than right here.

I didn't need—or want—to be anchored in a safe harbor

anymore, waiting for a new life to start. I was sailing by starlight and I was my own North Star. My dad, my friends, and Dax were bright, beautiful constellations in my universe to help me find my way.

I glanced around at my friends. *No longer alone.* My gaze slid over to Dax, and he must have felt it because he turned away from the football conversation and smiled at me with his bad-boy smile and hot eyes. *No longer invisible.*

"Hey, it's a close battle but the girls are ahead," Bhakti announced.

"Ali and Dax, you two are up," Mari said.

"You've got this." Gaby and Ro both fist bumped me.

"Dude, don't go easy on her because she's your girlfriend," Grady warned.

Dax and I moved up to the lanes, the ball return between us.

"You ready for this, gummy bear?" He grinned and threw in a wink for good measure.

"If you're trying to distract me, it won't work," I lied, extending my right hand over the air vent.

Dax put his hand next to mine, the cool air hitting both our palms. And then he wrapped his hand around mine, holding it tight.

EPILOGUE

Ali

May 21ST AKA LAST DAY OF SENIOR YEAR

"Hey, hi. It's been a while." Recording into my phone, I realized I hadn't updated my video diary since December. "Almost five months! I guess I've been busy. There's almost too much to talk about. But since this is going to be my last entry, I should give this chapter of my life closure.

"The Jackalopes made it into the championship game—and won! Yep. State Champs! Thanks to Dax and Rowena, everyone in school stopped blaming me for the playbook mess. Turk and his friend were suspended. Paige and Gwen were kicked off the cheerleading squad and no one talks to them. Not even Kev.

"Gah! There's too much to cover. Anxiety level: a zero and a ten. Zero anxiety in this moment, but a ten for all the changes ahead."

Exciting changes, but still...

"Today's objective: enjoy—"

"Enjoy hanging out with me," Dax said, jumping up next to me on the tailgate of his truck. He wrapped his arm around me and winked into the phone. "Hey, Ali. When you watch this in ten years, you should know you were wild about me."

"Stop." I laughed and bumped his shoulder with mine. "I'm trying to record my last diary entry for high school."

"Make sure you mention you won the girl's state finals and you're competing in the National Championship next month." Dax pointed into the phone. "You've got this, Ali Frost."

"Oh, Dax got a scholarship to his dream school. So, yeah, I'm dating a college quarterback."

Dax winced. "Yeah, like third string. Don't get excited until I'm the starter."

"I did *not* get a scholarship," I said. "Which, remember when I said a scholarship was the only way I'd be able to go away to college? Turns out there's another way. My dad went back to coaching."

"Man, the bidding war over him was crazy," Dax said. "He had, what, at least ten job offers? High school and college."

"Yep. He chose West Texas A&M University because I got accepted there. Which means…"

"Free tuition." Dax kissed my temple. "You'll only be two hours away from me at Tech. We're going to make this work."

"It'll be challenging, but I think you're worth it," I said.

"Ha! I wink at a challenge," he joked, but then his face went serious and intense. He wrapped my face in his hands. "Hey, I believe in us."

I smiled up into Dax's face, loving exactly where I was in this moment.

Dax leaned in and kissed me, leaving me breathless.

"I think you're still recording us," he whispered against my lips. Dax turned his face toward the camera. "Hey, Ali's diary. I told you that you were wild about me, Ali Frost. But that works out, because I'm wild about you too. Okay, let's wrap up, gummy bear. We've got graduation parties to get to."

"Yeah we do. So, that's a wrap." I stopped recording.

"And I was hoping to fit in a little stargazing... Think we still need to tell your dad we'll be at the observatory?"

"I think he trusts you, so no."

Dax jumped down from the tailgate, lifted me up, and spun me around.

"Whoa, getting dizzy up here!"

"Yeah, me too." He set me down gently. "Being around you has that effect."

Oh, yeah. This hot, crazy-good, not-very-beastly boy went right to my head.

"Ready?" His dark gaze—hot and fierce—locked on me as his hand wrapped firmly around mine telling me he was talking about more than parties and stargazing.

"More than ready. Oh! Hold on—I forgot one thing." Without breaking eye contact, I brought up my phone one more time. "Positive affirmation: The road is wide open and wonderful things are waiting ahead."

Thank you for taking the time to read *THE NERD & THE QUARTERBACK*. If you enjoyed it, it would be sweet if you have time to leave a review on Amazon. And I hope you'll stick around for the next installment in the Jackson High Series. Thank you! ♥ M.L.

HUGE HEARTFELT THANKS TO...

My parents, for being the best parents a girl could have wished for. (Mom, if there are libraries in heaven, check this one out. Not a single f-bomb. ♥)

My siblings, for putting up with me all those years. All the teasing, fighting, tutoring, laughing, and the "mom and dad love me the most"s made me the person I am today. My therapist thanks you. (*Kidding!*)

My husband, for *not* talking about building walls and trench drains just long enough so I could write this book.

My kids, for turning into upstanding, productive, responsible adults. I love you each the most!

To my Beta readers for reading through my not-very-pretty rough drafts. But, hey, it's not like I forced you to listen to me sing.

To my dog, for her loyal company in my writing cave. You deserve all the treats!

And to you, dear reader, for loving quirky sweet romances that make you snicker, swoon, and sigh.

ABOUT THE AUTHOR

M.L. Collins has done stuff. Good stuff. Bad stuff. Fun stuff. Boring stuff. She believes in true love, laughing loud and often, being kind, and assuming the best in people until they show you otherwise. She loves classic rock, old Motown, and '90s country music. She hates negative people, dill pickles, and scary movies. Loves windy days, dogs, and LOTR. She's an unashamed lover of sprinkles on cupcakes.

M.L. loves reading and writing quirky sweet romance novels that make you snicker, swoon, and sigh. She loves hearing from readers!

For more books and updates:
M.L. Collins website
M.L.'s Newsletter Sign-up

Printed by Amazon Italia Logistica S.r.l.
Torrazza Piemonte (TO), Italy

12549937R00132